Japanese-Style Gardens
of the Pacific West Coast

Japanese-Style Gardens
of the Pacific West Coast

Photographs by
Melba Levick

Text by
Kendall H. Brown

RIZZOLI
NEW YORK

To my Mother and Father with great love and much gratitude
—Melba Levick

First published in the United States of America in 1999 by

Rizzoli International Publications, Inc.

300 Park Avenue South

New York, NY 10010

Library of Congress Cataloging-in-Publication Data

Levick, Melba.
Japanese-style gardens of the Pacific west coast / photographs by Melba Levick ; text by Kendall H. Brown.
p.   cm.
Includes bibliographical references.
ISBN 0–8478–2109–9 (hc.)
1. Gardens, Japanese—Pacific Coast (U.S.)   2. Gardens, Japanese—British Columbia—Pacific Coast.
I. Brown, Kendall H. II. Title.
SB458.L48   1999
712.6'0952—dc21   98–48810
                                    CIP

Author's note: All Japanese names are given in Western form, with the family name last.

Designed by Border Editions

Printed and bound in Singapore

Contents

Territories of Play:
A Short History of Japanese-Style Gardens
In North America

by Kendall H. Brown

Artificial By Nature

At the turn of the century, and then again in the early 1960s, America witnessed a Japanese invasion in landscape architecture. So distressed by requests for a "Japanese garden" was garden designer James Rose that he spent much of his 1965 book *Gardens Make Me Laugh* chiding his countrymen for their infatuation with Japanese gardens. This was not a case of sour grapes by a cultural chauvinist: Rose—who had studied gardens in Japan—was a Harvard-trained landscape architect whose modernist work intersects aspects of Japanese design. For Rose, "A Japanese garden is a garden made in Japan. . . . There's no such thing as a garden where its people aren't. That's a *translation*, not a garden."[1] The American habit of reducing gardens—"explaining them away" with words—to design principles and symbolic metaphors is a way of bypassing the real human context and content of gardens. Rose also dismisses the issue of authenticity, writing that even gardens built in America by skilled Japanese landscapers, epitomized by Takuma Tono's 1962 recreation of the Ryōanji stone garden at the Brooklyn Botanic Garden, may "look like the real thing" but are not. Because the life of a garden depends on the way its makers thought about it, even old gardens in Japan are more dead than alive in the modern age. Moreover, Americans see differently from Japanese, speaking different "landscape languages." Because Westerners always use gardens differently from Japanese, the form of Japanese gardens in the West is inherently incongruous with their function. For Rose they are "museum pieces," no more alive than the stuffed dinosaurs in the Museum of Natural History. Attributing the vogue for these artificial gardens to a Western infatuation with Japan, Rose scolds Americans under the spell of Japan: "Why don't you take off that *mental* kimono? It looks silly. This isn't a masquerade. Or is it?"[2]

Rose's argument against nonindigenous design went largely unheeded by private and public patrons as the construction of Japanese gardens in the West increased dramatically from the mid-1960s through the 1980s. The postwar fascination for things Japanese equaled, if not surpassed, the prewar vogue for Japanese gardens, which was central to the broad cultural phenomenon of Japanism born in the late nineteenth century. It is no exaggeration to say that in the twentieth century more large-scale public "Japanese gardens" were built outside Japan than within. The great bulk of these are located in North America, particularly along the Pacific coast. Japanese gardens—or Japanese-style gardens, to extend Rose's reasoning—were ubiquitous in twentieth-century Western landscape design, spanning the globe from Wellington to Anchorage, Honolulu to Sophia. Three gardens constructed in the years just before the outbreak of World War II—when Japan's military aggression made its culture and the genre relatively unpopular—convey how deeply Japanese gardens penetrated the Western cultural landscape. In 1937, developer George W. Clark extended his own large, private garden in Jacksonville, Florida by adding oriental-style structures, bridges, lanterns, and other ornaments, and then opened it to the public as the "Oriental Gardens." In 1938 the Maharaja of Patiala imitated the fashion of great country houses in England by hiring a Japanese architect and landscaper to construct a garden with teahouse at his Motibagh Palace in northwest India. And, in 1939, when garlic pioneer Kiyoshi Hirasaki saw the large temporary pavilion and garden that the Japanese government constructed at San Francisco's Golden Gate Exposition, he decided to have part of the exhibit reconstructed next to a newly built garden at his residence in Gilroy, California, when the fair ended in 1940.

While a handful of landscape designers has adapted the essence rather than the external forms of Japanese gardens to fulfill Rose's idea of indigenous design, far more common has been the imitation of the obvious elements of Japanese gardens—the stone lanterns, torii gates, and arched bridges that appear in botanic gardens and apartment complexes, city parks and Asian restaurants. Despite the ubiquity and even beauty of some Japanese-style gardens, Rose's critique remains valid: most of these gardens are Japanese only in the most perfunctory ways. They may look reasonably Japanese, but they usually neither *feel* nor *act* Japanese. Even when gardens are used for such Japanese activities as the tea ceremony (*chanoyu*) or moon-viewing, the function seems stilted and unnatural—a revival or masquerade akin to an academic exercise or carnival attraction.

Gardens and Ghosts

In the West, and especially in America, where they are most often encountered, Japanese-style gardens exist as a kind of ghost. Japanese gardens are undoubtedly real: the originals are visited by millions annually in Kyoto and other Japanese locales; hundreds of books in Japanese, English, and other languages recount their history, dissect their symbolism and design, give advice on their construction, or simply provide photos testifying to their beauty. The desire to possess them has resulted in Japanese-style gardens in nearly every major city in North America as well as in many other places around the world. While their forms are generally as fixed as stones set in the earth, Japanese-style gardens are strangely vaporous in their meaning. Despite the substantial differences between the cultures which produced gardens in premodern Japan and in the modern West, Japanese-style gardens made in America (whether for an entrepreneur in San Francisco in 1894, an industrialist's wife in Pasadena in 1934, or by a civic board in San Jose in 1964) are often treated as equivalent to gardens made in Japan (whether for aristocrats in 700, Zen priests in 1500, or samurai lords in 1800). It is precisely this radical disjuncture between the form, rhetoric, and actual function of Japanese-style gardens that renders them ghosts—mysterious presences from the unseen past which manifest a physical likeness in our world.

Japanese-style gardens are also apparitional in that their meanings are largely fluid and ambiguous. If the ghost passes through time and through matter, the ostensible "essence" of the Japanese garden passes between cultures and contexts. Yet, that "essence," like the vaporous form of the ghost, is amorphous and vague. The Japanese garden haunts our collective imagination, yet we are not quite sure what to make of it. The Japanese garden becomes whatever we want it to be. From the first the Japanese garden—whether in Kyoto or Kansas City—has stood as a tangible antithesis to Western values. To quote one garden's pamphlet from about 1966, "An Occidental garden attempts to subjugate nature, an Eastern garden accepts it." Where most Western gardens are symmetrical and rational, the Japanese garden is asymmetrical ("each turning in a Japanese Garden path, designed for maximum enjoyment, provokes an aura of

mystery and quiet mediation").[3] A half-century earlier the sentiment differed little. In the words of two writers in 1916: "For the native of Japan, a garden is Fancy's Playground, a veritable place of romance . . . holding it as a retreat for contemplation and rest of mind. There associations must be friendly, there no rancor and strife of business must have place. It is, indeed, the lack of romance and mystery in our [Western] gardens which renders them so stupid."[4] The Japanese garden provides the locus of escape from the oppressive modernity of the West. As such, it must always be the ahistorical and essentialized Other, the mirror opposite by which the West both defines itself and seeks release.

Despite its static function as an emblem of the informal, natural space of the East in contradistinction to the formal, artificial space of the West, the idea of the Japanese gardens has evolved to parallel changes in Western design and thought. In the early twentieth century, when Victorian ideas were ascendant, Japanese gardens often represented quaintness and romance, the picturesque assemblage of materials for maximum decorative effect and moral edification. For Edmund Buckley, writing in 1908, "The expression of sentiment and morality widely differentiates the Japanese garden from its Western rival, which confines itself to a purely esthetic purpose. . . ."[5] With the rise of modernism in the mid-twentieth century, the Japanese garden increasingly embodied simplicity, the rejection of materialism, and a kind of philosophical purity. In his influential *Gardens in the Modern Landscape*, published first in 1934 and then again in 1948 and 1950, Christopher Tunnard argues that to find a technique for the contemporary garden, made to complement asymmetrically balanced modern architecture and to express an "affinity with nature," then "it is to the gardens of Kyoto that we must turn. . . ." For Tunnard, "When the sentimental, superficial approach to this oriental art through its merely decorative aspects has been abandoned by the Western mind it will be discovered that the underlying principles may very well serve as part of the basis for a modern technique."[6] Japanese gardens, "made to be seen sitting down," are marked by "extreme simplicity" with emphasis on "form, line and economy of material," "unity of the habitation with its environment," and awareness that man's "identity is not separate from Nature." Made to carry the ideological freight of its interpreters, in many ways "the Japanese garden" is figuratively a Western construct.

Japanese-style gardens are literally Western constructs. In the language of the spirit world, they are wraiths—apparitions bearing likenesses of the living as seen just before their deaths. Even as modernization was killing off premodern gardens in Japan, they were being reborn in the West. When still built in Japan, they are most often embalmed as remnants of tradition and known self-consciously as a *nihon teien* or "Japanese garden." And in the West they almost always bear the marks of reconstitution in a strange land. Although physically transformed in the process of rebirth, these so-called Japanese gardens retain the appellation of their forbears. Given their great numbers and often distinctive formal as well as functional differences from gardens in Japan, Japanese-style gardens constitute a distinct type of Western garden. Casting these modern gardens as identical to gardens of premodern Japan masks this most central fact of their existence. Although Japanese-style gardens appear most everywhere—a rooftop in Rockefeller Center, a community college in Midland, Michigan, a quarry in San Antonio—they remain phantoms. As "Japanese gardens" they hover dreamlike, beyond our grasp.

They cease to be specters only when we think of these gardens as one genre of Western landscape architecture, their history derived from that of the countries in which they were made and function. Japanese-style gardens materialize as real, living gardens when their ideology, purpose, and function are reunited with their form. No doubt this demystification drains much of the romance from these gardens. Because legend is more compelling than history, shadow more enticing than sunlight, it may be disappointing to think about such gardens as those in this book as American or Canadian gardens rather than Japanese ones. A Japanese-style garden in San Diego is less romantic than a "Japanese garden" in San Diego. Moreover, most of these gardens were built as "Japanese gardens," their rhetoric based on the illusion that when one gazes upon them, one sees Japan; that when one sets foot in a "Japanese garden," be it in Osaka or Orlando, one is in Japan. Central to the rhetoric of the ghost Japanese garden is the idea of "authenticity"—and most every Japanese-style garden claims to be authentic. One book on the principles of Japanese gardens deploys as examples only gardens in the United States. Its basic premise is that spiritual serenity is the essence of gardens in Japan, but because few Americans visit those gardens, they may substitute the "Japanese gardens" in America, which "recreate the Japanese style and provide a venue for experiencing" this spiritual type of landscape.[7]

This book, in contrast, presents Japanese-style gardens on the Pacific coast of the United States and Canada as flesh-and-blood North American gardens rather than as specters of Japanese gardens. In James Rose's terms, it elucidates the "what" of the gardens by returning them to the people who built, funded, and used them. As such it is little concerned with the symbolism or design theory of Japanese gardens. Rather, each of the twenty gardens is discussed in terms of its place in the evolution of Japanese-style gardens, patronage, relation of function to design, and use. These mundane concerns do not deny the beauty or tranquillity found in these gardens. Beauty and tranquillity are better experienced than discussed—and the photos do a very good job of suggesting what words strain to achieve. The experience of the gardens becomes richer when we begin to understand their often complex histories. We make these gardens multidimensional when we take into account the people who struggled for their creation and the people who have deployed them. We bring them more fully alive when we consider their designs not merely the recreations of Japanese prototypes but as the creative acts of designers translating the style of one time and place into very different temporal and spatial dimensions. And we give the gardens real significance when we see them as part of the cultural context of North American attitudes toward Japan.

"Japan" in America

When one culture creates forms and entire places based on those of another culture, and then pretends that the creations are authentic—the real thing rather than recreations—far more is revealed about the culture doing the action than the one being acted upon. Japanese-style gardens in North America tell us more about America and Canada than they do about Japan. As opposed to merely being "Japanese," the gardens evince their patrons' and consumers' particular attitudes toward Japan. In essence both the gardens and their functions present a type of orientalism through which Westerners literally and figuratively construct the Orient of their imagination by exaggerating some aspects of Asian culture while ignoring others. In orientalism, Asian culture is read through the filter of Western desires and fears. These gardens, and their histories, reveal fundamental aspects of a century of North American political, economic, and cultural relations with Japan.

Japanese-style gardens in their construction and consumption constitute one aspect of Japanism—the American cultural fascination with Japanese culture manifest in adopting and adapting aspects of it in art and architecture. In his groundbreaking 1964 book *The Japanese Influence In America*, Clay Lancaster traces in detail American architecture and garden design and, far more briefly, graphic art and decorative art in Japanese or "Japanesque" styles. While subsequent studies have focused on Japanism in painting, prints, decorative arts, and even architecture,[8] gardens have received little attention, apparently considered too close to Japanese models to merit extended analysis. But Japanese-style gardens were born among the cultural confluence that made popular the sketches and paintings of Japan by Robert Blum, the Japanese-theme prints of Helen Hyde, and the Japanesque architecture of Bruce Price and Frank Lloyd

Wright. In the postwar era, the rebirth of Japanese-style gardens took place in the same culture that produced the Japanese-derived architecture of Richard Neutra, the sculpture of Isamu Noguchi, and the painting of Mark Tobey. Where artists and architects often produced work based on their own discrete experiences and interests, and often for small numbers of patrons, most Japanese-style gardens were produced through group efforts and intended for a broad public audience. Part of popular culture, they are directly connected with the vogues for Japan which swept through America in the decades around 1900 and then again in the years since World War II.

Nothing epitomizes America's initial infatuation with Japan as clearly as Madame Butterfly, a cultural phenomenon that kept the romantic "Japanist" view of Japan at the forefront of the American cultural consciousness for more than two decades. In 1895, John Luther Long published Madame Butterfly, the most popular of his five novels about Japan.[9] In 1900 in New York and then in London, producer David Belasco turned it into a successful play which in 1903 was adapted by Giacomo Puccini into the famous opera. In 1915 director Adolph Zukor made the story into a movie starring Mary Pickford and filmed in the Japanese-style garden of Phiroz D. Saklatavala in Plainfield, New Jersey. Madame Butterfly not only spawned imitators in all artistic forms, but was the direct inspiration for at least one Japanese-style garden—that of Isabel Stine, a founder of the San Francisco Opera Company who staged a performance of Madama Butterfly in Hakone, her Japanese-style garden near San Jose. The tale of the wife who sacrifices herself was so closely associated with Japan that in 1934 when the Japanese American daughter-in-law of Gorō Hagiwara—proprietor of the Japanese Tea Garden in Golden Gate Park—killed herself and her infant son by taking a match to their gasoline-drenched bodies, the San Francisco Call reported, "The wind in the trees hummed a requiem—like a plaintive refrain from 'Madame Butterfly'—as old Gorō, tears in his eyes, stumbled back to the house."[10]

Less than a decade after the end of World War II, America had rediscovered its infatuation with Japan. But this time the direct experience of many occupation soldiers and their dependents gave Americans a direct and ostensibly more sophisticated knowledge of Japanese culture. By about 1960, Japan was on the itinerary of countless Western writers touring "the Orient." Again popular literature on Japan was ubiquitous, seemingly every writer having his or her say on the culture and, invariably, the gardens. Gardens figure prominently for instance in Nikos Kazantzakis's 1962 study of Japan entitled The Rock Garden, Ian Fleming's 1964 James Bond adventure You Only Live Twice, set in a Japanese "suicide garden," and Pierre Boulle's 1965 novel Garden on the Moon, in which a Japanese scientist builds a rock garden on the lunar surface.[11] An early example of the postwar rediscovery of Japan was Vern Sneider's 1951 novel The Teahouse of the August Moon—turned into a Pulitzer Prize–winning play

in 1953, then a film in 1956—in which Americans set out to teach democracy to Japan but end up the students of Japanese culture, as symbolized by a teahouse with garden: "Fisby made a mental note to notice and appreciate, then settled back to contemplate his surroundings. He breathed deep, looked at the small pines, looked at the cha no yu house resting beneath their overhanging branches, and nodded. Yes sir, it was a fine thing, a garden like this. If more people did it, there wouldn't be so many ulcers and nervous breakdowns. It did something for your system. . . ."[12]

Fascination with Japan was not confined to art and literature, but was translated into design styles appropriate for American homes and gardens. Of the many books, pamphlets, and articles on Japanese aesthetics and landscape architecture, few were as thorough or as influential as the two issues of House Beautiful published in August and September 1960. The first, devoted to Japan and bearing the issue title "Shibui, the word for the highest level of beauty," explores the Japanese aesthetics of simplicity and naturalness in architecture, gardens, and other arts. The next issue, "How to be shibui with American things," details many ways in which Americans may adapt Japanese design in their own homes, gardens, and daily life. In contrast to the "quaint and charming" image of exotic Japan prevalent in the prewar decades, characterized here as the "passing passions for miniature gardens, paper parasols, and lanterns," this new wave of Japanese influence was promoted as a more perceptive understanding of the spiritual depths of Japanese culture. For landscape design this usually meant integration of interior and exterior space, asymmetry or irregularity, emphasis on natural materials and effects, muted colors, and a feeling of informal elegance. Japanese garden design was considered ideal for standard suburban houses because it could create a sense of spaciousness and serenity using modest materials. Adapting ideas from David Engel's 1959 book Japanese Gardens For Today, articles in the magazine advised Americans in the utilization of fences, rocks, water, and ornaments in the spirit of Japanese aesthetics.

Even as the modernist taste for Japanese design was translated by House Beautiful, Sunset, and other magazines into a new suburban garden style, and simultaneously manifested in a fashion for "Zen-style" rock-and-sand gardens, both for residences and the public, there also remained the earlier fascination with Japan as the "flowery kingdom" of quaint teahouses and charming women. Madama Butterfly, for example, continued to draw audiences and haunt the imaginations of American women. The 1953 sweepstakes winner in Pasadena's Rose Parade was the "Madam [sic] Butterfly" float sponsored by the city of Glendale, which later built a Japanese-style garden. At Descanso Gardens in neighboring La Canada, in 1960, the women of the Descanso Guild decided to construct a Japanese garden and for their initial fund-raiser hired a UCLA opera troupe to perform the first act of Madama Butterfly. Similarly, when the Lotusland garden in Montecito, California, staged a 1995 fund-raiser in its

Japanese garden, the theme was "Lotusland Celebrates Twilight With *Madama Butterfly*." The romance, exoticism, and femininity still associated with Japan and its gardens was perhaps best expressed in 1966 when the Federated Garden Clubs of Birmingham, Alabama, held "Operation Kimono," or "K-day," in which club women in colorful kimono stood on downtown street corners soliciting donations for the Japanese garden at the Birmingham Botanical Garden.

In the postwar decades the image of Japan became increasingly complex, as it was dually associated with the chrysanthemum, representing the feminized artistic culture symbolized by Madame Butterfly, and the sword, denoting the ascetic, masculine culture of Zen. Both aspects of Japanese culture found expression in gardens—often at the same time. Increasingly after 1960 these two images were juxtaposed in single gardens which sought to demonstrate not merely the range of Japanese garden styles but to subsume the culture itself by encapsulating its polarities. Nathan Glazer argues that American attitudes toward Japan have been shallow and hastily formed, resulting in contradictory impressions bolstered by the paradoxical character of Japanese culture. Sheila Johnson, in contrast, contends that American conceptions of Japan are situational, changing in response to historical situations.[13] The evidence of Japanese-style gardens suggests that Americans have found in Japan a text whose value lies not so much in what the Japanese have written into it, but rather in the range of meanings Americans may read from it. Japan is thus not so much a given text to be decoded, but a text that is constantly being written. Japanese culture is so compelling because it can be interpreted differentially, meaning virtually whatever best suits a particular audience. Thus the staggering number of Japanese-style gardens—including from 1967 to 1974 a full-scale Japan-themed amusement park, the Japanese Deer Park and Village in Southern California—testifies not merely to the variety and depth of Japanese culture but to the creativity of American culture, which has repeatedly sought, found, and even built the Japan it desires. Japanese Americans and Japanese have often been complicit in this process of fashioning "Japan" in America.

Japanese Americans

Japanese-style gardens do not exist against the "background" or within the "context" of American attitudes toward Japan; rather, they are active agents in creating those attitudes. Moreover, the gardens—like the attitudes—are created not by a homogenous entity known as "Americans" but by individuals. While many of the persons instrumental in the fabrication of gardens were of European descent and long resident in America, they rarely constructed Japanese-style gardens alone. For example, even the kimono-clad, donation-gathering ladies of Birmingham's Federated Garden Clubs were joined by local Japanese women. And the idea for the garden came from Japanese "war bride" Reiko Parsons, who, stricken with an inoperable brain tumor, returned to Japan to die, leaving her husband and young children in Birmingham. Her final request was that a garden be built so they, and all children in the area, would grow up in the presence of something Japanese. The garden was designed by Buffy Murai, a San Francisco–born and Tokyo-raised man who had served as advisor for *Sayonara* and several other films set in Japan. The original teahouse at the garden was donated by the Japanese government after building it first at the 1964 New York World's Fair. The garden was a collaborative effort between the Caucasian establishment in Birmingham, Japanese Americans and Japanese.

It is the rare Japanese-style garden in North America, whether public or private, that was not built, financed in part or whole, maintained, or used by persons of Japanese ancestry. For Americans and Canadians of Japanese descent, the Japanese-style garden has been an important space of cultural production. Gardens are a crucial part of the immigrant experience for many ethnic Japanese in the West, integral in terms of economics and the politics of identity. Japanese-style gardens have frequently served as the most tangible aspect of cultural identity, at times stating Japaneseness and in other instances modifying that identity to represent Japanese Americans or Japanese Canadians. For Japan, Japanese-style gardens have often served as congenial symbols for the most attractive aspects of the nation. As such they have been utilized as long-term cultural ambassadors.

In both the pre- and postwar periods, most large Japanese-style gardens were designed and constructed by Japanese or first-generation (*issei*) Japanese immigrants. In the last decades of the nineteenth century and the first decades of the twentieth century, virtually all Japanese-style gardens were the result of the planning and physical toil of issei men. It is one of the seeming paradoxes of Japanism that garden construction flourished at precisely the time when Japanese immigrants were barred from becoming citizens and, in western states, prohibited from owning land. The "yellow peril" of Japanese immigration was so feared in California that in 1920 James D. Phelan, former governor and founder of the Japanese Exclusion League, ran for the U.S. Senate on the slogans "Save Our State From Oriental Aggression" and "Keep California White." Ironically, Phelan's great estate, Villa Montalvo, near Saratoga, was flanked on the north by Isabel Stine's Japanese-style estate, Hakone, and on the south by Max Cohn's Japanese-style garden, Kotani'an. For such Japanophiles as Stine and Cohn, a Japanese-style garden was emblematic of their interest in Japan and perhaps of their distance from the Eurocentrism of men like Phelan. However, it is likely that most Caucasians who strolled through the Japanese-style gardens at worlds fairs or in civic parks were fascinated with Japanese culture but still uncomfortable with the idea that Japanese people were their equals. Aware of both the hostility facing them and of the popularity of Japanese-style gardens, Japanese immigrants built gardens as a way of smoothing the path of acceptance in American society by emphasizing the most attractive manifestation of their culture. For instance, in the 1930s in California, Japanese American students and their parents built Japanese-style gardens at Sierra Madre Elementary School in Sierra Madre, Roosevelt High School in east Los Angeles, and Sequoia High School in Redwood City. And, in 1931, a Japanese business organization in the Sawtelle district of west Los Angeles contributed a small civic garden dedicated "to the Public for the Promotion of Better Understanding."

For many issei, building gardens served as a way of defining their Japaneseness and of maintaining ties to the homeland left behind, but also as a means of securing a living and even assimilating into their new country. For proprietors of commercial tea gardens like Makoto Hagiwara—a former restaurateur and, reportedly, brothel owner who ran the Japanese Tea Garden in Golden Gate Park from 1895 to 1925—Japanese culture was largely a commodity. In this regard Hagiwara differed little from his rival George Turner Marsh, who between 1896 and about 1930 built a half-dozen commercial Japanese gardens as part of his oriental antiquities business. Yet for such early-twentieth-century garden builders as Kinzuchi Fujii, Tokutarō Katō, and Takeo Shiota, who worked as farmers, carpenters, or florists to support their families between garden contracts, the Japanese garden was a labor of love by which they simultaneously defined and refined their Japanese identity even as they achieved some measure of success in America. While Katō and Shiota maintained pure Japanese styles, mid-century landscapers like Fujitarō Kubota and Shōgo Myaida (who altered the spelling of his family name so non-Japanese could more easily pronounce it) attempted to adapt Japanese design to the culture in which they lived. When new issei like Nagao Sakurai, Kōichi Kawana, Kimio Kimura, and Takeo Uesugi came to America after the war, they similarly sought to reconcile their patrons' usual desires for "authenticity" and their own interests in landscapes that, like themselves, bridged the two cultures.

Japanese-style gardens were not only built by Japanese Americans, but built for them as well. In the 1930s several successful issei—including flower farmer Zenjūrō Shibata in Hayward and garlic pioneer Kiyoshi Hirasaki in Gilroy—hired Japanese carpenters and landscapers to help them construct Japanese homes and gardens which eased their adjustment to life permanently in America and marked their preeminent status in the Japanese community. In some cases these large residential gardens were sites for picnics and other issei social events. In the years just before Pearl Harbor, the Fukunaga family in central Los Angeles opened their large garden (figure 1) for the annual photos of the princesses chosen for Nisei Week, a newly instituted Japanese American festival. Even when Japanese Americans were relocated away from the Pacific coastal regions in the wake of Pearl Harbor—most forcibly sent to hastily built camps in inhospitable desert locales—garden building continued. In most camps the industrious internees turned desert wasteland into bountiful fields and made life more

figure 1.
The Fukunaga family garden in Los Angeles
served as a backdrop for Japanese American community events
in the years just before World War II.

figure 2.
*The garden of the Fukuda family
at the Minidoka Relocation Camp, Idaho,
is one of many gardens built by internees
intent on beautifying
the barren camp environment.*

bearable by forming clubs for everything from Nō drama to swing music. In the camps at Gila River in Arizona, Manzanar and Tule Lake in California, and Minidoka in Idaho (figure 2), where water, plants, and rocks were available, internees built Japanese-style gardens of several types. The flimsy and faceless barracks were often beautified with stones, plants, and even lanterns fashioned out of recycled materials. In communal areas larger gardens featuring waterfalls, ponds, and sometimes stone bridges were lovingly constructed, usually by men who had worked as landscapers, gardeners, or nurserymen. Preserved in a few photographs and the piles of stones which stand as mute reminders of the once vibrant camps, these gardens made familiar the strange land, boosted the esteem of men deprived of their livelihoods, and symbolized the endurance of Japanese Americans in the face of great injustice. Jeanne Wakatsuki Houston describes the effect of looking through a garden at Manzanar toward the crest of the Sierra Nevada: "You could face away from the barracks, look past a tiny rapids toward the darkening mountains, and for a while not be a prisoner at all. You could hang suspended in some odd, almost lovely land you could not escape from yet almost didn't want to leave."[14]

After the war, as Japanese Americans reformed communities and community pride, Japanese-style gardens were built again. Buddhist churches often featured arrangements of pines, stones, and lanterns to signal the congregation's culture. In a few instances, most notably at Buddhist temples in San Jose and Anaheim, full-fledged gardens were made by parishioners in the landscaping business. More emblematic than aesthetic, they parallel the gardens in the yards of many second- and third-generation Japanese Americans intent on preserving their heritage and signaling their presence to the larger community. In some neighborhoods, Chinese and Vietnamese immigrants have imitated these designs—the ubiquitous front-yard lantern and clipped pine becoming a pan-Asian symbol of ethnicity in America. In contrast to these implicit messages, other gardens explicitly enunciate or commemorate Japanese American presence and history. For instance, in 1965 San Joaquin County Japanese Americans built a three-acre garden with teahouse and large pond in Micke Grove Park in Lodi,

California. To celebrate the Canadian centenary in 1967, the Japanese Canadian Citizens' Association in Vernon, British Columbia, constructed a garden in Poulson Park. And, at the small pavilion and garden constructed in 1970 at the courthouse in Santa Ana, California, a commemorative plaque reads: "Dedicated and presented for the pleasure of all people in Orange County by the Japanese American community. A grateful arigato in honor of our pioneer fathers and for the blessings of freedom." In 1979 the Japanese American Cultural and Community Center in the Little Tokyo section of Los Angeles constructed a garden, its three-part watercourse representing the experiences of three generations of Japanese Americans. A Japanese-style garden was built in 1984 on the Salinas Rodeo Grounds, a former relocation assembly center, as part of the redress movement that sought and eventually won a formal government apology for the internment of Japanese Americans. And, in 1990, the Oregon Nikkei League sponsored Robert Murase's design at the Japanese American Historical Plaza in Portland. Composed of a series of stones inscribed with Japanese and English haiku poems on the Japanese immigrant experience and the pain of the relocation camps, this "garden" stands as a powerful testament to the defining event in Japanese American history by using a design which synthesizes Japanese stone gardens and modern Western sculpture—an appropriately multicultural style for a Japanese American monument.[15]

Most of the pre- and postwar issei landscape builders were Japanese citizens. Some settled permanently in North America, often becoming American or Canadian citizens when finally offered the chance, while others eventually returned to Japan. In the competitive world of Japanese-style garden design, the Japanese birth and training of these men were integral to the authenticity typically desired by public and private patrons who sought a "real Japanese garden" for their estate or municipality. Because many early issei garden builders had only limited experience in Japan, American patrons often boosted their own status by falsely claiming that their man was "an Imperial gardener" or inventing some other impressive pedigree. Even more "authentic" than the Japanese immigrant was the Japanese designer commissioned directly from Japan, preferably recommended by the Japanese government or with a university teaching position. As Japanese-style gardens increased in status as the twentieth century wore on, the status of the designer grew in importance. For designers born in America, whether Japanese American like Robert Murase or Caucasians like David Engel, David Slawson, or Ron Herman, a stint in Japan—ideally studying at a major university and apprenticing with a famous Japanese "master"—was nearly requisite in terms of both professional skill and social status. Publishing a book that demonstrated one's training was also an effective way of establishing credentials. Because the rhetoric of Japanese-style gardens conceives of them as Japanese gardens, the basic calculus is that the closer the designer to Japan, the greater the authenticity of the garden.

Japan and America

Despite the dominant discourse on authenticity, on adherence to a putative Japanese tradition, Japan has not simply played the role of the passive original to be copied. The Japanese government, both at the local and national levels, has been active in the construction of Japanese-style gardens abroad. Japanese industry has also played a key role in the foreign dissemination of Japanese landscape design, usually in the form of money contributed to various funding bodies. Most public Japanese-style gardens built between 1950 and 1998 have been aided in part by contributions of money, materials, or labor from Japanese government or business. Roughly half are sister city or friendship gardens in which a Japanese municipality typically helped in supplying materials. In some cases, however, the Japanese city proposed the garden, designed it, provided most materials, and then built it with workers from Japan. Even when the Japanese city contributed only a commemorative stone pagoda or lantern, the fact that the garden is sanctioned by or connected with Japan is key to its rhetoric as a "Japanese garden." In several cases—the Kaizuka Garden in Culver City, California, and Kasugai Garden in Kelowna, British Columbia—the garden is named after the affiliated Japanese town. The Japanese-style garden has provided Japanese cities, and the nation as a whole, with a relatively cost-effective type of long-term advertisement for the aspect of its culture most accessible to and popular with foreigners. Symbolically, gardens embody economic and political relationships. Moreover, at times when tensions denigrate Japan's image internationally, gardens are an effectively indirect way of creating a positive impression. The beauty, serenity, and age-old tradition of gardens countermand the threatening image of the modern industrial nation and economic competitor trumpeted in newspaper headlines. Even though the great majority of sister city and friendship gardens has been initiated from the North American side of the Pacific, Japan has usually been active in their creation. While these gardens are typically marked by the pastiche design and cliché Japaneseness characteristic of the orientalist fantasy of Japan, Japan itself has often played a role in creating and sanctioning this fiction.

While Japan's role in international affairs in the modern period may well be described as masculine—based on economic strength after the war and on military power before it—the face presented to the world via gardens was very much a feminine one. The first Japanese gardens outside Japan were those sponsored by Japanese government and industry at international expositions. At early expositions— Vienna in 1873, Philadelphia in 1876, and Paris in 1878 and again in 1884—the Japanese government contributed relatively small exhibits with nominal "gardens" that were casual arrangements of plants, fences, and lanterns. Despite their rudimentary form, these gardens and accompanying teahouses or other structures effectively implied that Japan was a country of quaint charm ever devoted to its tradition of craftsmanship. By the end of the nineteenth century, Japan realized that the growing scale and number of international expositions provided a unique opportunity to influence world opinion at the time when Japan's burgeoning industrial and military power was transforming the nation into an international power—a position gradually confirmed by Japan's victories in the Sino-Japanese War of 1894–95, the Russo-Japanese War of 1904–05, the so-called Manchuria Incident of 1931, as well as the 1937 invasion of China.

With the 1893 World's Columbian Exposition in Chicago, Japan began the construction of major pavilions and gardens as well as massive displays in the halls of commerce, industry, agriculture, and education, becoming at most fairs the largest foreign exhibitor. In sharp contrast to its displays of modern technology and industry in the neoclassical exhibition halls, the Japanese government chose to build its national pavilion, the Hōōden, in a historicizing style, adapting the famous eleventh-century Hōōdō of the Byōdōin temple near Kyoto by combining architectural features from the three historical periods thought to best characterize premodern Japanese culture. The structure was surrounded by garden paths winding through thousands of plants brought from Japan. Another garden, with stone lanterns and bronze cranes, flanked the Nippon Tea House. When the Japanese government—then at war in Korea—sat out the 1894 California Midwinter Exposition in San Francisco, Australian entrepreneur G. T. Marsh won the rights for the Japanese

Village (later the Japanese Tea Garden in Golden Gate Park). This loss of ability to represent their own culture, and to prosper from doing so, outraged local Japanese businessmen, who soon built a rival tea garden at the fair.

At the Louisiana Purchase Exposition of 1904 in St. Louis, Japan created the sensation of the fair with its 175,000-square-foot compound (figure 3) composed of six "traditional" structures: the Formosa Tea Pavilion (representing Japan's newest colony), the Bellevue Tea House (sponsored by the Central Tea Grower's Association), the Bazaar, Main Pavilion, Commissioner's Residence, and a "replica" of the famous late-fifteenth-century Golden Pavilion in Kyoto. In the center was the Imperial Japanese Garden, also called the "Enchanted Garden," which included an island, arched bridge, iron and stone lanterns, bronze cranes, a variety of blooming plants, and a small teahouse where women served tea. The original plan was for a replica of Nagoya Castle with a small teahouse, but the outbreak of the Russo-Japanese War forced a new plan ostensibly to save money. The more peaceful arrangement of temple-style wooden buildings around a large stroll garden elicited the desired response. In the 1904 article "Some Of The Reasons Why Americans Like The Japanese," Isaac Marcossan explained: "In arrangement and detail the national pavilion shows that, to the achievement of commerce and industry, the Japanese have brought the perfection of landscape beauty, another expression of the genius of a people who, in the art of war and the pursuits of peace, are steadily making their way to a large place in world power. For this is the real significance of the Japanese exhibit in St. Louis."[16]

The Japanese government also deployed exposition gardens in response to regional political concerns. When the organizers of the 1915 Panama-Pacific International Exposition in San Francisco invited Japan to participate in 1912, the government accepted, aware that by skillfully presenting Japanese culture they might offset anti-Japanese sentiment. However, when Californians pressed ahead with the Alien Land Act, banning Japanese from land ownership, Japan withdrew from the fair. Dismayed at the loss of the largest and most popular foreign exhibitor, the fair's backers—San Francisco's leading businessmen—tried to persuade the legislature to postpone a vote on the bill until after the fair. Conservative politicians and newspapers in turn railed against the "tea garden," their shorthand for Japan's participation. James Phelan proclaimed, "Japan may not [choose to] exhibit at our fair, but we cannot sell our birthright for a tea garden." And a *Sacramento Union* editorial opined, "We believe [labor] desires the Japanese burden off its shoulders just as much as it ever desired it, and that it will not be lured from its opposition by promise of the most beautiful tea-garden that the mind of Oriental man has conceived."[17] Japan eventually did participate, building a display similar to that in St. Louis. It featured an entry gate, commissioner's office, two very successful teahouses, and a reception hall bastardizing the Golden Pavilion and housing a miniature replica of the temples at Nikkō. Roughly half the Japanese space was filled with the "Imperial Japanese Garden," composed of a pond, red bridge, rest pavilions, stones, lanterns, bronze Buddhist statues, bronze storks, and hundreds of imported trees and shrubs. Despite the hostility of many Californians toward Japanese immigrants, most visitors were charmed by the "fairy garden" inhabited by winsome Japanese maidens. Isabel Stine, a devotee of Puccini's *Madame Butterfly*, was so taken with the teahouses that after the fair closed she took a trip to Japan and then commissioned a Japanese house and garden, Hakone, at her estate on the east side of the Santa Cruz Mountains. After the fair William Sesnon, a major exposition backer, and his wife, a member of the women's auxiliary board, also built a Japanese-style garden at their estate in Aptos on the west side of the Santa Cruz Mountains.

Japan's next large-scale garden participation at American expositions came in the 1930s when the Japanese military and political intervention in Manchuria and northern China in 1931, and subsequent invasion of southern China in 1936, antagonized American public opinion. Japan initially declined to participate in Chicago's 1933 Century of Progress Exposition, citing economic depression and her concerns in Manchukuo—the name given to the newly created puppet state, not recognized by the U.S. However, Japan decided to participate when China planned a large pavilion and Chicago businessman William Bendix erected a replica of the Temple of Jehol—a building from an area disputed by the Japanese and Chinese. Although the American government and corporate pavilions as well as those of the few European exhibitors were in the streamline modern style, the Chinese and Japanese built in pseudo-historical styles. The Japanese pavilion featured a teahouse with small tea garden and a main pavilion with entry garden built by Tarō Ōtsuka, a Japanese living in Chicago who had constructed gardens throughout the midwest. Adjacent to the main pavilion was the South Manchurian Railway Hall where the Japanese, in violation of U.S. State Department warnings, attempted to convince fair-goers of their benevolent interest in Manchukuo, disseminating information on military and economic affairs amid kimono-clad maidens, cherry blossoms, and a peaceful garden.

In 1939, as Europe was plunged in war and Japan was bogged down in its "holy war" in China, large expositions opened in New York and San Francisco. Again Japan was one of the few foreign participants. In San Francisco the government erected a stylistically hybrid pavilion broached by a gently arched bridge spanning one corner of a large pond set with stones and decorated with lanterns. The image of serenity and natural beauty established by the exterior landscape was paralleled by interior displays focusing on silk production, culture, tourism, and traditional crafts. In a tearoom visitors could sip tea while gazing at a rock garden. More blatantly propagandistic was the facade of timeless beauty conveyed by the self-consciously traditional garden

figure 3.
Composed of five major structures
and a large pond-style stroll garden,
the Japanese compound
was the largest foreign display at the
Louisiana Purchase Exposition,
St. Louis, 1904.

figure 4.
Meant to evoke an image
of "changeless, timeless Japan,"
the Japanese pavilion and garden
sharply contrasted with
the "World of Tomorrow" theme of the
1939 New York World's Fair.

and architecture in New York (figure 4). Although the fair's theme was "The World of Tomorrow," manifest in the futuristic Trylon and Persiphere, the Japanese pavilion was an updated version of an ancient shrine, fronted by a rather prosaic garden constructed by Shōgo Myaida, a Japanese who had built gardens in the New York area since 1922. The official Japanese poster summarized the ideology of this pavilion and indeed all those at previous expositions: "Changeless, timeless Japan . . . its enduring charm takes its place naturally in 'The World of Tomorrow.' Visit the Japanese pavilion—a red-white-and-gold replica of a lovely Shinto Shrine—with its exquisite art treasures and displays. Rest awhile in the unique Garden, symbolic of Japan's varied landscapes. When the Fair's modern world bewilders you, remember—and enjoy—the Japanese pavilion!"

In the expositions after World War II, Japan adopted modernist design for its pavilions and attached gardens, abandoning the unrepentant historicism of the earlier temple-style structures and large stroll gardens. Now, the gardens—like the structures—were designed to suggest the fusion of Japanese tradition with high modern style. At Seattle's Twenty-first Century World's Fair in 1962, the simple, flat-roofed, steel-girdered Japanese pavilion contained a small rock-and-sand garden. Two years later at the New York World's Fair, the even more minimalist stone-clad Japanese pavilion designed by Kunio Maekawa included a rectangular, exterior garden courtyard containing abstract stone sculptures and a square central pool from which both nonrepresentative sculpture and natural stones emerged. Relative to this extreme abstraction, the pavilion and garden at Montreal's Expo '67 marked a far more conservative approach, seeking to synthesize the minimalism of modern design with the more overtly beautiful aspects of Japanese design. A hybrid garden occupied an area between the third and fourth parts of the four-section pavilion. In its center was a pond fed by a stone-lined stream meandering across a grass lawn. At the edge of the pond a broad "beach" of white gravel was set with stones as well as beds of white and red flowering ground cover. The aesthetic dissonance of this hard-edged abstraction and the more traditional stream suggested a radically condensed version of the multistyle Japanese-style gardens then being built in the United States.[18]

While gardens at postwar international expositions had little impact, those of the late nineteenth and early twentieth centuries had a tremendous influence on Japanese-style garden building in North America. First, these gardens were seen by millions of visitors and experienced secondhand by millions more who read about them in newspapers and gazed at photos in magazines and illustrated books. Second, the gardens were seen in the context of the fairs, which, for all their entertainment value, were largely considered educational events. Sponsored by the Japanese government, these gardens bore the official imprimatur of the Japanese authorities as well as the gravity of the expositions. Third, most gardens extended their life beyond the several months of each exposition. The Japanese government often maximized the public relations potential of its exhibitions by donating its pavilions to the host city—an act which not only saved the cost of transporting the buildings and garden ornaments back to Japan, but also obviated the need to pay tax on these commercial import goods. As a result of this largesse, civic Japanese gardens were established in Chicago from 1893, San Francisco from 1895, and San Diego from 1915. Some gardens, particularly the Japanese Tea Garden in Golden Gate Park, were so commercially successful that they launched a vogue for commercial tea gardens, which brought public Japanese-style gardens to all corners of North America. Finally, because of the temporary nature of exposition buildings and gardens (including those in the commercial entertainment sections), when the fairs ended, objects not donated locally were often sold to individuals or businesses. For instance, a teahouse from the 1965 New York World's Fair ended up in Birmingham, Alabama; the silk display room from the 1939 Golden Gate exposition became part of the Hirasaki residence in Gilroy; and in 1908 the monumental gate from the "Fair Japan" concession in St. Louis was moved to Fairmount Park in Philadelphia, where it anchored a newly built garden commemorating the Japanese garden at the 1876 Philadelphia Centennial Exposition. When the gate burned in 1955, park authorities received as a gift the formal, "proto-modern" Japanese residence designed for display in 1954 at the Museum of Modern Art in New York. The display house's rock-and-pond garden was not transported to Philadelphia, so in 1957 Tansai Sano and David Engel built a large pond garden—Fairmount Park's third Japanese-style garden in eighty years.

These temporary exposition gardens, both in original design and in subsequent reconstruction, reveal an active process of making history and culture, a process that lies at the very heart of each Japanese-style garden. The Japanese exposition commissioners, private individuals, and park boards who recycled garden structures, ornaments, and even plants, were in effect playing with the past: plundering a millennium of Japanese landscape and architectural styles, they created gardens that—like Dr. Frankenstein's monster—were new forms combined from various old parts. The literal, physical transportability of garden elements parallels the less obvious but just as real historical transpositions at play when styles from the fifteenth and eighteenth centuries are revived in the twentieth century in gardens that claim, and are generally believed, to be "authentic Japanese gardens." Japanese culture, processed for malleability and portability, has found ready consumers in North America and equally eager producers on both sides of the Pacific. This orientalizing, or self-orientalizing, commodification of culture represented by the Japanese-style garden is based on the idea that gardens can be made to represent the Japanese historical past by collapsing or synthesizing it into a single entity capturing the essence of Japanese culture.

This plundering of the past is based on a view of history that notes differences yet finds an essential core of values. The gardens at the international expositions between 1867 and 1967 testify to a Japanese conception of landscape and indeed cultural history based on a relationship with the West that seeks to isolate and demonstrate a Japanese uniqueness antithetical to the values of Europe and America, but also to uncover the universality of Japanese culture as an equally critical component of its relationship with the West. Japanese garden scholarship in the late nineteenth and early twentieth century was largely concerned with historical texts on garden design and theory. This focus on design principles and aesthetic values is evident in studies of the eleventh-century *Sakuteiki* (Notes on Garden Making), the fifteenth-century *Senzui narabi ni yagyō no zu* (Illustrations for Designing Mountain, Water, and Hillside Field Landscapes), and the eighteenth-century *Tsukiyama teizōden* (Creating Landscape Gardens),[19] as well as in the many books on Japanese garden history. The discreet sociopolitical implications of gardens have received little attention until very recently.[20]

Because the forms of Japanese garden design have not been rigorously viewed as determined by specific historical circumstances, they have been ideologically and functionally free-floating, applicable whenever and wherever they can again be of service, no matter how disparate the original and subsequent uses. At Chicago, in 1893, the Hōōden pavilion adapted the eleventh-century Hōōdō, but the garden made no reference to either the pond-based aristocratic or Pureland-sect Buddhist gardens of the Heian period (798–1184), both of which were inextricably linked formally and functionally with the Hōōdō. Rather, in Chicago the Japanese designers created the informal stroll garden associated with restaurants of the late nineteenth century. Indeed, while the architecture of the early Japanese-style gardens in the West is usually historicized, the gardens tend to follow the rather ornate and synthetic landscape taste of the Meiji period (1868–1912). At the 1904 St. Louis and 1915 San Francisco fairs, the Japanese displays mixed architectural adaptations of the late-fourteenth-century Golden Pavilion with landscaping based on Edo-period (1615–1868) stroll gardens associated with samurai lords, or *daimyō*. The large scale and opulence of the style fit not only late Meiji taste but also the ambiance of the exposition where nations strove to impress with profusion rather than restraint. Moreover, at a time when Japan's military exploits were generally well regarded in the West, the connection made by the architecture and gardens with the shoguns or *daimyō* of Japan's military heritage carried few negative implications. In the smaller gardens built by Japan for the 1930s expos in Chicago, San Francisco, and New York, the landscape was far more intimate. Made to be seen either from within the pavilions or as an adjunct to the architecture when viewed from outside, but never to be entered, these gardens were based loosely upon Edo-period temple gardens. This choice may stem from the quasireligious architecture of the Chicago and San Francisco pavilions and the restricted space of all three plans. At the postwar expositions, when Japan sought to

figure 5.
A copy of the fifteenth-century
Silver Pavilion in Kyoto was
the focal point of
the Japanese Tea Garden at
Piedmont Park in Oakland, California,
ca. 1900.

distance itself from the prewar style and ideology yet maintain its fusion of uniqueness and universality, the abstract modernity of the sand-and-stone gardens associated with Zen temples was an obvious choice.

Despite the different styles and historical models, the exposition gardens were all alike in that each was deracinated, its style uprooted from the nurturing functional and theoretical soil in which it was born. The styles that grew out of the Zen culture of the sixteenth century or from military society in the eighteenth century now represented not so much the values of the priestly or warrior communities, but rather Japan in sum. And this Japan—as it exists in the West and vis-à-vis the West—is, at heart, about ahistorical essences.

North American Garden Types and Functions

The few exposition gardens had a tremendous impact on the hundreds of Japanese-style gardens in North America. Most resemble the exposition gardens in that they generically represent Japan, yet differ because they were not constructed temporarily at the "tournaments of nations," but were built in a wide range of locations to perform a variety of specific functions. And, most importantly, they were usually built by North Americans. Thus these gardens are American or Canadian in both context and function, growing out of the histories of these countries and revelatory of them. The great majority of Japanese-style gardens in the West can be classified as commercial, residential, civic, or cultural. Some cut across categories. For instance, exposition gardens were simultaneously commercial (directly and indirectly selling Japan and Japanese products), civic (gestures of international goodwill), and cultural (meant to teach about Japan). Investigation of Japanese-style gardens within the rubric of these functional categories foregrounds the role of these gardens in North American life. It also illuminates the sociopolitical dimensions of these gardens and indeed the underpinnings of Japanism.

The early exposition gardens had their most immediate impact on North American garden building in terms of commercial tea gardens. The tea pavilions at the fairs in Chicago, San Francisco, and St. Louis, as well as those in Buffalo, Portland, and Seattle, were so successful economi-

cally that both Japanese and American entrepreneurs sought to mimic them with commercial tea gardens. In some cases they used the actual structures or plants and ornaments from the Japanese exposition displays. Most gardens were located in resort areas, often at or near large resort hotels where guests sought new sights and experiences. The Japanese-style gardens were exotic—and often slightly erotic due to the presence of kimono-clad women—but safely so. With little effort, risk, or money relative to traveling to Japan, visitors to commercial gardens could feel that they had traveled to a strange, new culture. Because of these functions, it was crucial that the gardens promote themselves as authentic no matter how spurious the claim.

The earliest public Japanese-style garden was likely at a resort in Blair Park in Piedmont, California. Built in 1891 as part of a complex featuring canals and a planned casino, it had lilies, a wisteria arch and a teahouse staffed by Japanese "maidens" in "full native costume." A larger rival garden (figure 5)—boasting a replica of Kyoto's late-fifteenth-century Silver Pavilion, a small pond garden and a hedgerow maze with a pagoda at its center—was constructed around 1900 in nearby Piedmont Park. Far better known is San Francisco's Japanese Tea Garden at Golden Gate Park, an offshoot of the Japanese Village at the 1894 California Midwinter International Exposition. It was run by businessman Makoto Hagiwara from 1895 to 1900, and from 1907 until his death in 1925. From 1900 to 1907 Hagiwara was barred from the garden and, in retaliation, opened the San Francisco Hagiwara Tea Garden near the park. The tea garden at the 1893 Chicago World's Columbian Exposition had been managed by the enterprising Yumindo Kushibiki. The venture was so successful that in 1897 Kushibiki and several partners opened a six-acre commercial tea garden near Boardwalk and Massachusetts Avenue in Atlantic City. After this huge garden closed in 1900, with many of its structures going to private gardens around Philadelphia, Kushibiki opened a tea garden on the rooftop of Madison Square Garden in New York. Featuring Japanese waitresses in "native costume" and a replica of Mt. Fuji, the garden hosted such light opera as *The Mikado* and heavy drama as the murder of famed architect Stanford White in 1906. The latter reportedly

A-59   HOLLYWOOD — FROM BERNHEIMER'S GARDENS, HOLLYWOOD, CALIF.

boosted business more than the former. Other commercial tea gardens were run by Kōhachi Handa at Pacific Point near Monterey, California, from circa 1904 to 1918; by Joe Kishida and Harry Takata at Gorge Park in Victoria, British Columbia, from 1907 to 1942; and by Kimi Jingū at Breckenridge Park in San Antonio from 1918 to 1942.

The king of the commercial tea garden was oriental antiquities dealer George Turner Marsh. Marsh, who built the Japanese Village at the 1894 San Francisco fair, constructed a string of tea gardens including a small one at the Hotel Green in Pasadena in 1896, a three-acre garden in Pasadena in 1903 (bought by Henry Huntington in 1911), a large garden erected in 1906 across from the Hotel del Coronado, and from around 1910 a miniature garden at Mission Cliff Park, also in San Diego. The G. T. Marsh and Co. shops in San Diego and Monterey featured courtyard gardens built in the 1920s. And, from 1895, Marsh turned his rural weekend home on Mt. Tamalpais in Mill Valley into a Japanese-style retreat, converting buildings from the Village at the Mid-Winter Fair into bungalows. The complex also included a Japanese open-air wooden bath—Marin County's first hot tub. Nippon Mura, a similar Japanese-theme resort, was built in 1901 in Saratoga by Theodore Morris.

Several hotels across North America featured tea gardens. Notable prewar examples include the Redondo Hotel near Los Angeles, the Huntington Hotel in Pasadena, the Mission Inn in Riverside, the Spring Hotel in French Lick, Indiana, and a rooftop garden at the Ritz-Carleton in New York. Although small Japanese-style gardens were constructed at upscale Japanese restaurants from the 1950s, it was not until the late 1960s that the style was considered sufficiently elegant to appear again at major hotels and resorts. The quasi-Japanese gardens at the Century Plaza Hotel in Los Angeles, Lodge of the Four Seasons at Lake Ozark, Missouri, and the Pagoda Hotel in Honolulu are among the earliest. From 1970 Japanese-theme gardens and architecture appeared at budget motels in the west, countless hotels in Hawaii, and Japanese-owned hotels including rooftop gardens at the New Otani in Los Angeles, Miyako Hotel in San Francisco, and Hotel Nikko properties in Atlanta and Chicago. Japanese-style gardens even turned up

at such unlikely locations as the Radisson Inn in Plymouth, Minnesota. Related to hotel gardens are large restaurant gardens, which, in theory, not only suggest the authenticity of the cuisine but transform the experience of the meal into an ersatz trip to Japan. The advertising copy for one famous Los Angeles restaurant with a Japanese-style garden reads "Only minutes away, but a world apart." Representative examples include the elaborate stroll gardens at the Gasho restaurants in Central Valley, Hawthorne, and Hauppage, New York. In Greenville, South Carolina, the Nippon Center Yagoto presents a spectacular sand-and-stone garden visible to diners as well as a large stream garden near the entrance. In stark contrast, Benihana Japanese Village—with talking Buddhas and singing birds—at the Las Vegas Hilton revels in faux exotica that is tacky even in Las Vegas.

Another offshoot of the early commercial tea garden was the large-scale attraction garden, a forerunner of the modern theme park. The earliest and greatest of these gardens were built by Adolph and Eugene Bernheimer. Oriental antiquities dealers from New York, the brothers moved to Los Angeles in 1912 and began to build Yamashiro in the Hollywood Hills. Featuring a twenty-two-room Japanese-style house, which held their art collection, the surrounding garden included a two-story pagoda, gate, and small pavilions as well as a miniature Japanese garden (figure 6). Sold in 1922, it became a private club, a private residence, a boys' school, an apartment house, and is currently a restaurant. In 1925, in Pacific Palisades, Adolph Bernheimer built the Bernheimer Japanese Garden, touted as "Where the Orient meets the Occident." Featuring a Japanese-style gate and residence perched on cliffs above the Pacific, the spacious garden grounds were planted with exotic flora, dotted with oriental statutes, and included miniatures of various Asian architectural wonders on an island in a pond. The Bernheimer Garden was a casualty of World War II, which also spelled the demise of Eagle's Nest Japanese Gardens in Clearwater, Florida. Built in 1938 by Dean Alvord, the huge property included paths with torii gates, shrines, bridges, lanterns, thousands of flowering plants, a five-story pagoda, and a teahouse where kimono-clad women served tea and food.

figure 7.
Replicas of the pagoda
at Hokkōji in Nara Prefecture
and the Silver Pavilion in Kyoto
announce the Japanese theme
of Kyoto Gardens Memorial Park,
Honolulu, Hawaii, 1966.

After the war the commercial potential of Japanese-style gardens reached its apogee. In 1964, Murata Pearl Company opened Murata Pearl Village at Sea World in San Diego. The Village revolved around a lake where female pearl divers from Japan dove for small pearls set in oysters. Visitors could then have their pearl set in jewelry at the gift shop, an adaptation of the ever popular Golden Pavilion. The Japanese ambience of the compound was created by a stroll garden around the lake as well as by a dry garden in one corner. Even more grandiose was the Japanese Village and Deer Park in Buena Park, from 1967 to 1974 providing very slight competition for nearby Knott's Berry Farm and Disneyland. Featuring animal shows, tame deer, and demonstrations of Japanese cultural activities including tea ceremony and martial arts, the Japanese architecture and garden struggled to create the ambience of Japan. The same combination of entertainment and commerce distinguishes the Japanese section of the World Showcase at Disney's EPCOT Center in Orlando, where a Mitsukoshi department store is set in a Japanese-style garden. At the other end of the scale are the small "Japanese gardens" at such southern commercial gardens as Jungle Gardens of Avery Island, Louisiana; Bellingrath Gardens near Mobile, Alabama; Mynelle Gardens in Jackson, Mississippi; Ladew Topiary Gardens in Monkton, Maryland; and Cypress Gardens in Winter Haven, Florida.

Japanese-style gardens have also been built to enhance other types of businesses. After Hubert Eaton created the concept of the memorial park at Forest Lawn in Los Angeles, rival cemeteries responded by constructing Japanese-style gardens to create a positive and peaceful environment for visitors. In the formerly segregated cemetery world, a Japanese-style garden suggested that the property was open to Asians. In contrast to the decidedly meager Japanese elements of the garden built in 1959 at Rose Hills in Whittier, California, the 1966 Kyoto Gardens Memorial Park in Honolulu (figure 7) offers a garden setting with "replicas" of the three-story pagoda at Hokkōji in Nara and the Golden Pavilion. Even more elaborate is the Byōdō-in Temple at The Valley of the Temples, also on Oahu. Focused on a concrete replica of the eleventh-century Hōōdō or Phoenix Hall near Kyoto, the complex is approached by a red bridge spanning a koi-filled pool and also includes a meditation house and waterfall.

The serenity and timelessness associated with Japanese gardens make them appropriate for cemeteries. The same qualities inspired Deborah Szekely to choose the style in 1975 when she began rebuilding her famous Golden Door spa near Escondido, California. Adapting the architecture and landscape design of the Japanese *honjin* inn—those reserved for the most distinguished guests in the Edo period—Szekely created a world of tranquillity, naturalness, and spirituality for clients willing to spend thousands of dollars for a week of mental and physical rejuvenation. At least one developer and several corporation presidents sought to lure clients to office parks or to increase employee productivity by building Japanese-style gardens at office complexes. While Gulf States Paper in Tuscaloosa, Alabama, was the first of these corporate gardens when built in 1970, the most elaborate is developer Jack Naiman's 1982 San Diego Tech Center. Japanese companies have also used Japanese-style gardens to distinguish themselves. The trend among Japanese corporations in North America for Japanese-style gardens began in the mid-1960s when expatriate landscape designer Eijirō Nunokawa fashioned gardens for Japan Airlines at Los Angeles International Airport and for Seibu department store on the roof of its Wilshire Boulevard building. In the 1970s the North American divisions of the auto-makers Nissan and Mazda included small gardens at their corporate headquarters south of Los Angeles in order to comfort Japanese executives transferred to a foreign land and to soften the threat posed by Japanese corporations in America. The garden donated by the Brother Corporation to Bartlett, Tennessee—part of the company's "good neighbor policy"—presents a variation on the earlier model.

Japanese-style gardens have also been part of cultural institutions, primarily museums and universities. Because modern museums often seek to present art within the context of its culture, several museums have featured Japanese-style gardens. In 1909 the Museum of Fine Arts in Boston constructed galleries for its superb Japanese art collection around a courtyard featuring a pond garden. After the pond leaked in the late 1950s—almost ruining the collection of Nō robes stored below it—a dry rock garden took its place. Five years after this was removed, when the galleries were remodeled in 1982, Kyoto garden designer Kinsaku Nakane was selected to build the lavish Tenshin-en garden next to the museum's new I. M. Pei–designed West Wing. Outside the lobby of the Pei-designed East Wing of the National Gallery in Washington, Nakane erected a small stone-and-gravel garden in 1988. Planned as a temporary addition for a Japanese art exhibition, the abstract garden was so well adapted to the architecture that it became part of the permanent design. Interpreted as being virtually analogous to modern sculpture, the stone garden appears at such museums as the Peabody Museum in Salem, Massachusetts; the Huntington Library, Art Collections and Botanical Gardens in San Marino, California; and the Canadian National Museum of Civilization in Hull, Ontario. In Florida, Japanese-style gardens grace the Academy of Four Arts in Palm Beach, the Ormond Beach War Memorial Art Gallery, and the Morikami Museum in Delray Beach. Visitors to the Los Angeles County Museum of Art approach the Pavilion for Japanese Art by a bridge passing over a garden composed of elements—rustic gate, stone basin, lanterns—characteristic of the *roji* or tea garden. A chief attraction of the Carter Presidential Center in Atlanta is Kinsaku Nakane's dramatic waterfall garden of 1982, donated by the Japanese zipper manufacturer YKK. According to a plaque, the "magnificent and dignified" large waterfall represents President Carter while the smaller waterfall symbolizes "the beautiful Mrs. Carter."

Universities have demonstrated their internationalism or multiculturalism by means of Japanese-style gardens since at least the early 1920s, when the University of Missouri erected a torii gate on a pond island and Breneau College in Gainseville, Georgia, hired Shōgo Myaida to design a Japanese-style summer camp. From these humble beginnings the vogue for Japanese gardens accelerated rapidly after 1960, when the University of British Columbia built the large Nitobe Memorial Garden. In the early 1960s pond gardens were built at the Oberlin Conservatory of Music in Ohio, Delta Court Community College in Saginaw, Michigan, and Furman University in Greenville, South Carolina. In 1963 controversy swirled around the Japanese garden at the East-West Center of the University of Hawaii in Honolulu when, in response to an open invitation for American landscape architects to join in its construction, modernist designer Garrett Eckbo wrote a letter to the journal *Landscape Architecture* stating his reasons for declining: "A Japanese garden can only happen in Japan. Anywhere else it is an imitation Japanese garden."[21]

In a July 1964 article in the same journal, other landscape architects rallied to the defense of "the Japanese garden" as a living art relevant to modern Western viewers—particularly at institutions of higher learning. This view prevailed in the late 1970s and early 1980s as gardens were made at Normandale Community College in Minnesota, the University of Alberta's Devonian Botanical Garden, Haverford College in Philadelphia, California State University at Long Beach, and the nearby California State University at Dominguez Hills. In the following decade David Slawson created gardens based on Japanese principles for Carleton College in Northfield, Minnesota, and for Smith College in Northampton, Massachusetts, while Stephen Morrell designed a Japanese-style garden behind the Center for East Asian Studies at Wesleyan University in Middletown, Connecticut. According to their pamphlets, these gardens teach students about Japanese culture. More importantly, they symbolize the institution's cultural sophistication even as they beautify its physical environment. As such, these gardens share the rhetoric and function of Japanese-style gardens constructed by cities and towns across North America.

Civic gardens are so numerous that only a brief overview is possible here, with several stellar examples discussed in the following sections. Whether built at botanical gardens, arboreta, city parks, or as independent sister city gardens, civic gardens in most North American cities constitute part of the urban landscape—encountered as frequently as zoos or drive-in theaters. The genre boomed in the 1960s and 1970s, but even before World War II a dozen or so gardens sprang up in the wake of expositions and commercial tea gardens, usually the gift of a benefactor or the special project of a city official. However, because these gardens were not constructed with community support, most quickly succumbed to neglect or were destroyed during the war as part of the "war at home." For instance, in January 1942, when the city fathers of Memphis voted to bulldoze the

"Japanese Garden" in Overton Park (figure 8), a local newspaper headline wryly announced "Memphis Japanese Garden Falls Without A Shot Fired."

The Memphis garden was built by Park Commission chair Col. Robert Galloway in about 1905, the Colonel explaining that "it will do more for the schoolboy or -girl than any other feature, for it will stimulate interest in a country that will not stop at the Japanese village." Like many prewar gardens it featured a replica of Mt. Fuji. Other pond-style gardens from the 1900s include those built in St. Paul's Como Park and Philadelphia's Fairmount Park. The next decade saw the creation of civic gardens ranging from the exotic orientalism of Bradley Park in Peoria, Illinois, to Takeo Shiota's magnificent "Japanese Garden" at the Brooklyn Botanic Garden. In the 1920s a small garden was constructed at the courthouse in Midland, Michigan, by Takuma Tono, who had just built a residential garden for local chemical magnate Herbert Dow. More typical were the gardens at Terrace Park in Sioux Falls, South Dakota; Swinney Park in Fort Wayne, Indiana; and Fairmount Park in Riverside, California. Despite the chill in Japanese-American political relations after the Manchuria Incident of 1931, the first years of the 1930s witnessed an increase in civic Japanese-style gardens. Examples include gardens in Roger Williams Park in Providence, the Oriental Garden in Jacksonville, the Jewel Box at Forest Park in St. Louis, Roeding Park in Fresno, Liliuokalani Park in Hilo, and, most dramatically, at the horticultural center atop the RCA Building at Rockefeller Center in Manhattan.

By 1975 Japanese-style gardens had become part of the fabric of North American cities, appearing either as manifestations of sister city arrangements, exotic sections of botanical gardens, or simply in municipal parks. For botanical gardens and arboreta, a Japanese-style garden offered a fitting location for Asian plants, a type of mysterious yet somehow familiar "natural" landscape architecture, and, in many regions, a way of involving the local Asian community with the institution. Japanese-style gardens at botanical gardens range from the large and elaborate to mere token efforts. Modest but skillfully designed gardens at botanical gardens include those in Nashville, Atlanta, Norfolk, Denver, Chanhassen (near Minneapolis), and Cleveland. Elaborate Japanese-style gardens are found at the botanical gardens in Fort Worth, Birmingham, and Seattle. Best-known are those designed by Kōichi Kawana in Chicago, Memphis, and St. Louis. Seiwa'en ("Garden of Pure, Clear Harmony and Peace") at the Missouri Botanical Garden in St. Louis, the largest Japanese-style garden in North America at fourteen acres, demonstrates the complex parentage and political ramifications of many civic gardens. Conceived in 1972 by Japanese Americans in St. Louis to honor their issei forbears, the Japanese American Citizens' League, Japan America Society, St. Louis-Nagano Sister City Organization, and local ikebana societies were all involved in its creation; funds were also provided by the Japan World Exhibition Commemorative Fund, the National Endowment for the Arts, and the Missouri Department of Natural Resources.

JAPANESE GARDEN, OVERTON PARK, MEMPHIS, TENN.   52

figure 8.
Built at the turn of the century,
the public Japanese Garden at Overton Park in Memphis, Tennessee,
was bulldozed just one month after Pearl Harbor.

As of 1995, 308 American municipalities and a large number of Canadian cities had sister city relationships with Japan. For both Japanese and North American municipalities, sister city gardens advertise their virtues. While Japanese cities use gardens to present a vision of historical tranquillity to counteract their image of modern vitality, for North American cities the sister city garden is a way of announcing their internationalism and receptivity to cultural diversity. For both sides, gardens cement human connections—good intentions and noble words transformed into stones and plants—but they also reflect local political and economic agendas. Sister city gardens have been generated from three sources: the Japanese city, Americans or Canadians of European descent, and Japanese Americans or Japanese Canadians. Some sense of the vast number of sister city gardens can be gleaned by citing examples of the three types from gardens built in the southern part of California in the mid-1970s. After Culver City hosted women's volleyball players from its sister city, the people of Kaizuka repaid the favor by designing a small garden, which was then transplanted by six Japanese workers to a rectangular space in front of the Culver City library in 1974. In the same year, the Higashi Osaka Garden was built in Glendale's Brand Park. Although many persons contributed to the teahouse and garden, the driving force behind the project was Anabel Neufeld, who, after her first husband's death in World War II, determined to show that nations could coexist peacefully. In 1968 several members of the Japanese American community in Fresno felt a Japanese garden would effectively represent their heritage. After forming a garden committee, and establishing a sister city relationship with the city of Kōchi, in 1974 they began work on the Shin Zen "Friendship" Garden in Woodward Park.

The final type of civic garden is that built in public areas but not at botanical gardens or generated out of sister city arrangements. Typically the product of North American civic groups, the leading example is surely the Japanese Garden of Portland—the result of Portlanders' desires to strengthen economic ties with Japan and beautify their city. Some gardens have been entirely funded and constructed by city governments. The Japanese Garden at the Tillman Water Reclamation Plant, dedicated in 1984 in the San Fernando Valley of Los Angeles, was created by the municipal water district of Los Angeles to demonstrate the use of reclaimed water and to assuage local residents who objected to a sewage treatment facility by their homes. The Japanese (and Chinese) gardens built in 1968 at the Honolulu International Airport provide a calming diversion for passengers while also proclaiming the city's rich ethnic mix. One example of the rare civic garden generated in Japan is at the Admiral Nimitz State Historical Park in Fredericksburg, Texas. When the founders of the museum—which commemorates the life of American Navy Admiral Chester Nimitz and is largely dedicated to America's defeat of Japan—expressed a desire for some Japanese contribution to the museum, in 1976 Japanese leaders donated a "Garden of Peace" composed of a stone-and-sand garden flanked by a reproduction of Japanese Admiral Heihachirō Tōgō's study pavilion. Related is the Miami Friendship Garden (formerly the Ichimura Miami-Japan Garden, and before that the San-Ai-An Garden), given to the city of Miami in 1961 by Kiyoshi Ichimura, founder of Ricoh Corporation, as a token of his esteem for Miami in particular and America in general.

These civic landscapes present the most public examples of the Japanese-style garden and demonstrate its range of functions and patrons. Most gardens, however, were built not for the public but rather created for and by private individuals. Residential gardens provide the best barometer of how deeply Japanese-style gardens have penetrated North American culture. Beginning just before 1900, when the American elite were in the first throes of Japanism—constructing Japanese rooms and, among women, dressing in kimono—Japanese-style gardens began to appear wherever the very rich gathered: Bar Harbor, the Boston suburbs, Newport, Tuxedo Park, the north shore of Long Island, Philadelphia's main line, the north shore of Chicago, the San Francisco peninsula, the Oakland hills, Montecito, and Pasadena. They were commissioned by many of the great names in American commerce: Rockefeller, Gould, McCormick, Armour, Seiberling (founder of Goodyear), Mellon, Mayo, Huntington, and Crocker. They also distinguished the estates of the local gentry in most every city, from Larz and Isabel Anderson's "Weld" and Isabella Stewart Gardner's "Greenhill," both near Boston, to Samuel Mills Damon's "Moanalua" and Alice Cooke Spalding's "Noumealani" in Honolulu. Following the model of the European country house, where Japanese-style gardens were not uncommon, formal French and Italian gardens were usually planted closest to the house, with the Japanese garden set on a distant, low, and watery part of the property. These gardens demonstrated the wealth and sophistication of their owners. More importantly, perhaps, the exotica and nostalgia manifest in these gardens were likely born from a deep antipathy to modernism which found solace in the past and in foreign cultures.[22]

Like antimodernism, the vogue for Japanese-style gardens extended to the middle class. In California, most notably, the many Japanese gardeners coupled with a cultural orientation toward the Pacific meant that Japanese-style gardens were built on lots in the subdivided flatlands as well as on estates in the hills. According to California historian Kevin Starr: "Japanese garden design, together with the ubiquitous Japanese lanterns for outdoor lighting, became increasingly characteristic of domestic landscaping. A generation of Japanese gardeners . . . was slowly coaxing the garden landscape of the Southland into arrangements inspired by the land of the Rising Sun."[23] However, as David Streatfield notes, "despite the area's large Asian population, this was not a regional celebration, but a decorative fascination with the visually exotic and fantastic with little or no appreciation for the spiritual and intellectual dimensions that informed the authentic style."[24] A stellar example of this

Japanese Garden of a California Home.

figure 9.
This postcard of an unidentified
"Japanese Garden of a California Home"
reveals the early-twentieth-century vogue for
Japan in residential architecture and landscape.

decorativeness is provided in Eugene O. Murmann's 1914 book *California Gardens*, which lists three Japanese garden plans among its fifty models for gardens on "city lot, suburban round, and country estate." Murmann provides photos of Japanese-style gardens at unidentified bungalow courts—proof that craftsman-style bungalows and Japanese-style gardens were considered compatible. The synthesis of oriental and occidental architectural modes, epitomized in the homes of Charles and Henry Greene, was well matched by gardens adapting Japanese forms (figure 9).

Residential Japanese-style gardens were erected until the Japanese bombing at Pearl Harbor, and then, after a hiatus of about fifteen years, began to appear again in the mid-1950s. Once more the wealthy hired experienced landscape designers to create gardens on large estates. Good examples were provided during the late 1950s by Marjorie Merriweather Post's "Hillwood" in Washington, D.C.; in the mid-1960s by Barbara Hutton's "Sumiya" in Cuernavaca; and, in the 1990s, by cybermogul Larry Ellison's two homes near Palo Alto, the first adapting the garden of Katsura Villa to an existing Japanese-style home, the second refashioning the entire Katsura complex.[25] Far more common, however, were gardens at suburban houses (figure 10), made either by the owners or by professionals. Just as many prewar gardens were inspired by Josiah Conder's *Landscape Gardening In Japan*, the techniques, styles, and indeed impetus for postwar gardens were aided and abetted by copious magazine articles and such how-to books as Samuel Newsom's 1939 *Japanese Garden Construction* (republished 1988), Isamu Kashikie's 1961 *The ABC of Japanese Gardens*, *Sunset* magazine's 1968 *Sunset Ideas For Japanese Gardens* (revised 1972), Jack Kramer's 1972 *Gardening With Stone and Sand*, Wendy Murphy's 1979 *Japanese Gardens* (from the *Time-Life Encyclopedia of Gardening* series), Kiyoshi Seiki's 1980 *A Japanese Touch For Your Garden*, and Ortho's 1989 *Creating Japanese Gardens*.

In the 1960s the fascination with Zen led some homeowners to fill in swimming pools and then top them with sand and rocks or otherwise contrive a dry garden. More common have been koi ponds, vermilion bridges, stepping stones, and a few garden ornaments.[26] Some gardens utilize only a "Japanese touch" provided by a lantern, stone arrangement, or even the integration of interior and exterior spaces. In his forward to David Engel's 1959 *Japanese Gardens for Today*, architect Richard Neutra praises the spiritual and temporal aspects of Japan and its gardens, which present "an argument against our vaunted 'progress.'" Neutra finds a useful model in the "humanized naturalism" that dynamically integrates the geometry of modular homes with the "relaxed asymmetry of the garden. . . ."[27] At the close of the century, full-blown and self-proclaimed "Japanese gardens" thrive alongside gardens that, like Neutra houses, seamlessly translate Japanese design into a modern idiom.

The Pacific West Coast

Japanese-style gardens exist in staggering numbers across North America and around the world. According to a 1996 survey of Japanese landscape design firms, Japanese-style gardens have been constructed in India, Indonesia, Korea, Singapore, Thailand, Taiwan, China, the Philippines, Malaysia, Papua New Guinea, Australia, New Zealand, Abu Dhabi, Iraq, Saudi Arabia, Egypt, England, Austria, Switzerland, Germany, Holland, France, Belgium, Norway, Finland, Italy, Bulgaria, Colombia, Chile, Brazil, Peru, Cuba, Canada, and the United States.[28] While rare in most regions, in North America, and particularly along the West Coast, Japanese-style gardens have been built in such large numbers from 1890 on that they constitute an integral part of the region's landscape and its culture. Neutra, for instance, found Southern Californians "mentally footloose" and thus receptive to new things like modern architecture and Japanese design.

The west coast of North America also makes a fitting focus for a study of Japanese-style gardens because of the area's plentiful and high-quality extant public gardens. The gardens in this book were selected based on four criteria. First, with the exception of the Golden Door, which is open only to paying guests, the gardens in the following chapters may be visited by the public. Second, located in major urban areas, the gardens are conveniently accessed by residents of the area or seen easily on a garden pilgrimage. Third, these gardens are large in scale, relatively well designed and skillfully maintained, offering viewers a compelling aesthetic

experience. Finally, they constitute representative types in the history of Japanese-style gardens in the West, and thus are of historical as well as visual significance.

The twenty gardens presented here make up but a small number of the public Japanese-style landscapes easily accessed along the Pacific coast. The ubiquity and adaptability of the genre is witnessed in the following list of other public Japanese-style gardens, arranged geographically from south to north: Sherman Library and Gardens, Corona del Mar; Costa Mesa City Hall; Santa Ana Civic Center Japanese House and Garden; Anaheim-Mito Sister City Garden; California State University at Dominguez Hills; Rose Hills Memorial Park; Torrance Culture Center; Gardena City Library; Kaizuka Meditation and Friendship Garden, Culver City; Stoner Recreation Center, Los Angeles; Pavilion for Japanese Art, Los Angeles County Museum of Art; New Otani Hotel, Little Tokyo, Los Angeles; Ashiya Park, Montebello; Nachi Park, Monterey Park; City of Hope, Duarate; Descanso Gardens, La Canada-Flintridge; Higashi Osaka Garden, Glendale; Shin Zen Garden, Fresno; Salinas Rodeo Grounds Japanese Garden; Iwata Friendship Garden, Mountain View; Miyako Hotel, San Francisco; Lakeside Park, Oakland; Hakusan Sake Gardens, Napa; Micke Grove Park, Lodi; Shore Acres, Coos Bay, Oregon; Choshi Sister City Garden, Coos Bay; Western Treasure Valley Cultural Center, Ontario; Manito Park Nishinomiya Gardens, Spokane, Washington; Central Washington University, Ellensburg; Pt. Defiance Park, Tacoma; Japanese Garden, Olympia; Seattle University; Yao Park, Bellevue; Hatley Park, Victoria, British Columbia; Butchart Garden, Victoria; Friendship Garden, New Westminster; North Vancouver Japanese Garden; Kasugai Gardens, Kelowna; Poulsen Park, Vernon; and Restaurant Nikko, Anchorage, Alaska.

In his book *Magic Lands*, David Findley observes that for Americans in the twentieth century, the west did not represent "open space" as it had in the nineteenth century. Rather, the American west's "virgin cities" offered new types of urban space.[29] Due to their relative "placelessness," disattachment from community, and rupture from traditional symbols of spirituality, people in western cities were relatively free to explore cultures and landscape patterns different from those dominant in the eastern and midwestern states. The

Orient provided one important ingredient in the "mixturesque" urban style that reached its apogee in California. Along with elements of fantasy adapted from the dreamscape architecture of Disneyland and Las Vegas, Japanese-style gardens have helped create the western city as a place of recreation and fantasy where one seems to walk not just in new kinds of spaces, but in other times and in other lands. In this sense, it is precisely because Japanese-style gardens have been cast as "Japanese gardens" that they "materialize escape" and thus fulfill so completely John Dixon-Hunt's idea that "gardens are territories of play—both play as alternative to work or business and play as theater, make-believe, the whole gamut of role playing that is human life. Though this last is not obviously confined to gardens, it flourished there because gardens are special sites of artifice pretending to be nature. . . ."[30] Because Japanese-style gardens are completely artificial by their very nature, they serve so well as "territories of play" within the Western culture that gave rise to them. Indeed this function necessitates the make-believe design and ideology central to the fantasy of the "Japanese garden" in the West.

Notes

1. James C. Rose, *Gardens Make Me Laugh* (Baltimore and London: The Johns Hopkins University Press, 1965), 53. The following discussion is from Part III, "Ah, Japan."
2. Ibid., 73.
3. "The Japanese Garden in Washington Park," pamphlet by the Japanese Garden Society of Oregon, ca. 1966.
4. J. Fletcher Street and Collier Stevenson, "Japanese Gardens in America," *House and Garden* (June 1916), 11.
5. Edmund Buckley, "Landscape Gardening in Japan," *House and Garden* (July 1908), 4.
6. Christopher Tunnard, *Gardens in the Modern Landscape* (London: The Architectural Press; New York: Charles Scribner's Sons, 1934; 2nd edition 1948, reprinted 1950), 81–92.
7. Maggie Oster, *Reflections of the Spirit: Japanese Gardens in America* (New York, Dutton Studio Books, 1993), 10.
8. See Julia Meech and Gabriel Weisberg, *Japonisme Comes To America: The Japanese Impact on the Graphic Arts 1876–1925* (New York: Harry Abrams, 1990); *The Japan Idea: Art and Life in Victorian America* (Hartford: Wadsworth Atheneum, 1993); and Kevin Nute, *Frank Lloyd Wright and Japan: Japanese Art and Architecture in the Work of Frank Lloyd Wright* (New York: Van Nostrand Reinhold, 1993). For a broader cultural study, see Ian Littlewood, *The Idea of Japan: Western Images, Western Myths* (Chicago: Ivan R. Dee, 1996). For a related study, see Tomoko Sato and Toshio Watanabe, eds., *Japan and Britain: An Aesthetic Dialogue 1850–1930* (London: Lund Humphries, 1991).
9. For an overview of Japanism in literature, see Earl Miner, *The Japanese Tradition in British and American Literature* (Princeton, N.J.: Princeton University Press, 1958).
10. "Kills herself, baby in flaming park pit," *San Francisco Call* (May 25, 1934), 1.
11. Included in this category are James Michener's 1953 *Sayonara*, John Marquand's 1957 *Stopover Tokyo*, James Clavell's 1975 *Shōgun*, James Melville's Superintendent Otani murder mysteries, and the "exotic intrigue" novels of both Eric Lustbader and Marc Olden.
12. Vern Sneider, *The Teahouse of the August Moon* (New York: G. P. Putnam's Sons, 1951) 196–97.
13. Nathan Glazer, "From Ruth Benedict to Herman Kahn: The Postwar Japanese Image in the American Mind," in Akira Iriye, ed., *Mutual Images: Essays in American-Japanese Relations* (Cambridge, Mass.: Harvard University Press, 1975). Sheila K. Johnson, *The Japanese Through American Eyes* (Stanford, Calif.: Stanford University Press, 1988).
14. Jeanne Wakatsuki Houston and James D. Houston, *Farewell To Manzanar* (New York: Houghton Mifflin, 1973), 72.
15. The garden is illustrated and discussed in Mark Sherman and George Katagiri, eds., *Touching The Stones: Tracing One Hundred Years of Japanese American History* (Portland: Oregon Nikkei Endowment, 1994).
16. Isaac Marcossan, "Some Of The Reasons Why Americans Like The Japanese," *The World's Work* (August 1904), 512.
17. James Phelan, quoted in Roger Daniels, *The Politics of Prejudice: The Anti-Japanese Movement in California and the Struggle for Japanese Exclusion* (Berkeley, Calif.: University of California Press, 1962), 60. "Labor Opposes Tea-Garden," *Sacramento Union* (January 11, 1913), 3.
18. For a survey of Japanese pavilions and gardens at international expositions, see Yoshida Mitsukuni, ed., *Bankokuhaku no Nihonkan* (Tokyo: INAX Gyararii, 1990). Smaller gardens were built by the Japanese government or business interests at expositions including those at Portland in 1907, Seattle in 1909, London in 1910, San Diego in 1915, and Philadelphia in 1926.
19. The three works are translated or adapted into English: see Shigemaru Shimoyama, *Sakuteiki: The Book of Gardens* (Tokyo: Town and City Planners, 1976); David Slawson, *Secret Teachings in the Art of Japanese Gardens* (Tokyo and New York: Kodansha International, 1987); and Josiah Conder, *Landscape Gardening in Japan* (London: Kelly and Walsh, 1893; reprinted New York: Dover, 1963).
20. The sociopolitical significance of gardens, present only at the margins of such otherwise fine studies as Loraine Kuck *The Worlds of the Japanese Garden* (New York and Tokyo; Weatherhill, 1968) and Günter Nitschke, *Japanese Gardens, Right Angle and Natural Form* (Cologne: Taschen, 1993), is broached in Wybe Kuitert, *Themes, Scenes, and Taste in the History of Japanese Garden Art* (Amsterdam: J. C. Gieben, 1988).
21. Garrett Eckbo, "Why a 'Japanese Garden' in Hawaii?" *Landscape Architecture* (January 1964), 89. In a follow-up

letter entitled "After Perfection What?" in the July 1965 issue of the same journal, Eckbo argues that because real design "is a specific creative process focused on the here and now," it is inappropriate to try to recreate garden styles of other countries and other historical periods.

22. For studies of American estates, antimodernism and gardens, see Clive Aslet, *The American Country House* (New Haven, Conn.: Yale University Press, 1990), T. J. Jackson Lears, *No Place of Grace: Antimodernism and the Transformation of American Culture 1880–1920* (New York: Pantheon, 1981); M. Christie Klim Doell, *Gardens of the Gilded Age* (Syracuse, N.Y.: Syracuse University Press, 1986); and Mac Griswold and Eleanor Weller, *The Golden Age of American Gardens: Proud Owners, Private Estates* (New York: Harry N. Abrams, 1991).

23. Kevin Starr, *Material Dreams: Southern California Through the 1920s* (Oxford: Oxford University Press, 1990), 190.

24. David Streatfield, "Western Expansion" in Massachusetts Horticultural Society, ed., *Keeping Eden* (Boston: Little Brown, 1992), 104.

25. Hutton's estate, featuring a pond garden and a Ryōanji replica, is published in *Architectural Digest* (September/October 1971), 9–21. Ellison's first garden is partially illustrated in Alan Deutschman, "The Next Big Info Tech Battle," *Fortune* (November 29, 1993), 38–39.

26. Several of these residential gardens are illustrated in Peggy Landers Rao and Jean Mahoney, *Nature On View: Homes and Gardens Inspired By Japan* (Tokyo and New York: Shufunotomo/Weatherhill, 1993).

27. Richard Neutra, forward to David Engel, *Japanese Gardens For Today* (Rutland, Vt., and Tokyo: Charles E. Tuttle, 1959), xi–xiii.

28. "Nihon no teienbi" ("The Beauty of Japanese Gardens") in *Niwa, The Garden* (October 1996), 133–136.

29. David Findley, *Magic Lands: Western Cityscapes and American Culture After 1940* (Berkeley, Calif.: University of California Press, 1992), 10.

30. John Dixon-Hunt, *Gardens and the Picturesque: Studies in the History of Landscape Architecture* (Cambridge, Mass.: MIT Press, 1993), 263.

Japanese Tea Garden at Golden Gate Park
San Francisco, California

The Japanese Tea Garden in San Francisco's Golden Gate Park is the oldest extant Japanese-style garden open to the public outside Japan. It is also the most visited— a San Francisco tourist attraction like Chinatown and Fisherman's Wharf—and undoubtedly the most famous Japanese-style garden in the West. For visitors who have never been to Japan, it likely represents all Japanese gardens. Some have praised its "authenticity" and many have waxed poetic on the serenity, spirituality, and purity ostensibly found here. But the Japanese Tea Garden's real richness is in its history: its complex politics and economics, the causes of its intense stylistic hybridity, and even the debate over its creation all highlight issues central to the hundred-year history of Japanese-style gardens in the West.

When oriental antiquities dealer G. T. Marsh (1855–1932) heard of M. H. de Young's plans for the 1894 Mid-Winter Fair in San Francisco, he applied for the right to the Japanese Village concession. Local Japanese businessmen and government officials soon protested, boycotting Marsh and building their own Japanese Tea Garden at the exposition. However, Marsh's one-acre "Village"—with teahouse, theater, arched drum bridge, ornate gate, and miniature garden—was so successful that when the fair ended, city legislators wished to keep the garden as a permanent part of Golden Gate Park. Marsh donated or sold most of his Village to the City, which then hired Makoto Hagiwara (1855?–1925) to run it as a commercial tea garden. Hagiwara, a Japanese restaurant owner and entrepreneur perhaps connected with the second Japanese garden at the fair, soon moved his family to a house in the garden, where they lived until May 1942. After Makoto Hagiwara's death, his adopted son and then daughter ran it until Japanese Americans were forcibly relocated from the Pacific coast in the wake of Pearl Harbor. One exception was the period from 1900–1907, when Hagiwara seems to have been barred from the garden, establishing a rival Japanese tea garden across the street from the park. During this period the city of San Francisco expanded the garden with a four-acre western

The bronze Buddha image, cast in 1790 in Tajima, Nara Prefecture, was donated in 1949 by S. & G. Gump Company.

section built around a large pond. This open area was augmented in 1915 when Hagiwara directed the transfer of a pagoda and temple gate from San Francisco's Panama-Pacific International Exposition. Added around the same time were a torii gate and Shinto shrine—the latter destroyed during World War II along with the Hagiwara house.

During the war, when the garden's name was changed to Oriental Tea Garden and the teahouse was staffed by Chinese women, Superintendent of Parks Julius Girod built a brick terrace and Sunken Garden on the area of the burned Hagiwara home. The pagoda was also moved to the site of the dismantled shrine—creating a syncretic arrangement where the Shinto torii leads to the Buddhist pagoda. In 1949 Alan Agnew became proprietor of the teahouse and gift shop, and the S. & G. Gump Co. donated a large bronze Buddha cast in 1790. In 1953, one year after the garden's name was changed back to Japanese Tea Garden, the Japanese Consul General presented a massive Lantern of Peace in the name of the children of Japan. In the same year, with political relations healing between the U.S. and Japan, Japanese landscape designer Nagao Sakurai was asked to build the so-called Zen Garden in a small, rear corner of the garden. Sakurai used two stones to represent a waterfall, gravel as a symbolic river, and created an island of moss with a small pine. In 1959, after Jack Hirose became concessionaire, the

The teahouse (previous page), although remodeled in 1959 by R. G. Watanabe, has remained a popular attraction since first installed in the Japanese Village at the 1894 California Mid-Winter Exposition.

The arched drum bridge (above) was built around 1912 to replace a similar bridge left from the original Japanese Village.

A stone pagoda (right) sits in the south side of the main pond, part of the five-acre expansion carried out around 1905.

The torii gate, pagoda, and temple gate,
originally built for San Francisco's
1915 Panama Pacific International Exposition,
dominate the north shore
of the main pond.

Japanese Tea Garden at Golden Gate Park

teahouse and gift shop were rebuilt. In the next year the San Francisco Garden Club hired Sakurai to reconfigure the pond area between the main gate and teahouse. Also in 1960 Porter Sesnon gave twelve stone lanterns, adding to an already rich collection. Upon departing in 1942, the Hagiwaras gave their bonsai collection to landscape designer Samuel Newsom, who, on their request, sold it to Hugh Fraser. When Fraser donated the bonsai to the garden in 1965, Newsom designed a hillside for them between the main pond and west gate. A Shinto ceremony celebrated the return of the collection. With the construction in 1966 of the Asian Art Museum wing of the de Young Museum adjacent to the garden, Assistant Park Superintendent Roy Hudson relandscaped the eastern part of the garden seen from the museum's windows. A rare boat-shaped water basin (*tsukubai*), given by the Gump Co. in 1966, was placed near the gift shop. Garden Supervisor Ed Schuster redesigned the pagoda area with a Buddhist theme in 1969.

Changes to the garden from around 1970 often were politically nuanced as developing Asian American consciousness led to a renewed appreciation of the Hagiwara legacy in the garden. First, in 1969, the Committee for Japan Week commemorated the centenary of the arrival of the first Japanese settlers in California by placing a large stone lantern outside the south gate. In 1974 a plaque honoring Makoto Hagiwara and his family was placed near the front gate, across from a 1960 plaque honoring Marsh. In 1979, just inside the main gate, Schuster created a conical hedge resembling Mt. Fuji to honor Makoto Hagiwara, who grew up near the mountain. And, by 1987 the city of San Francisco paid a small sum to compensate Hagiwara family members for their losses, officially acknowledged the Hagiwaras for "design, development and management" of the garden, and renamed the street fronting the garden Hagiwara Tea Garden Drive. Other amendments include the creation of the Maple Lane in the rear of the garden in 1977, and the reconstruction of the gates in 1985.

Despite the variety of its prolific structures, the beauty of its many shrubs and trees, and the charm of the numerous garden ornaments and vistas, at its heart the garden seems to be about people. Originally built as a village, the garden is still almost always full of visitors who sip tea at the teahouse, browse at the gift shop, climb the drum bridge and stroll the paths reading the many plaques and inscriptions, which convey much of the garden's long history. Beyond merely translating Japanese design principles and cultural values, this garden's most compelling story involves the many persons who built it, worked in it, and sought to interpret it. Far more than the arrangement of plants, water, rocks, and structures, the Japanese Tea Garden is the fluid product of American and Japanese ideas about how the image of Japan may function in North America.

The simple West Gate (overleaf), relocated by Fujimi Harazawa from the Japanese compound at the Panama Pacific Exposition, adds to the garden's hybrid aesthetic.

The Buddhist pagoda was moved to its current place next to the Shinto torii to replace the Shinto shrine dismantled during World War II.

Huntington Japanese Gardens
San Marino, California

The standard, modern rhetoric of Japanese gardens stresses a purity of conception and design. In contrast to this dominant image of the essential and timeless garden, many gardens have changed so greatly that their current state is but a shadow of the original. Even among the relatively young Japanese-style gardens in North America, many have been altered in appearance and some in function as well. The Japanese gardens at the Huntington Library Botanical Gardens in San Marino, California, demonstrate how for the past century Japanese-style gardens have kept pace with changing western concepts of Japanese aesthetics and spirituality.

After organizing the commercially successful Japanese Tea Garden for the 1894 San Francisco Mid-Winter Exposition, and in 1901 building a garden near the Hotel del Coronado in San Diego, G. T. Marsh expanded into Pasadena, where he opened a three-acre Japanese garden in 1903. When the garden went bankrupt in 1911 it was acquired for local railway and real estate magnate Henry Huntington by his horticulturist and ranch foreman William Hertrich. The two-story house, fence, arbor, bell tower, stone lanterns, statues, stones, and plants were moved to a ravine west of his great mansion newly constructed at Oak Knoll, where a reservoir was drained to create a koi pond and meandering stream. Huntington relocated the garden because of horticultural interest in its unusual plants, the pleasure of accumulating a new type of garden for his "collection," and to demonstrate to Arabella Worsham Huntington, the widow of his deceased uncle Collis P. Huntington, that the Southern California "ranch" was sufficiently civilized for her to marry him and move west. For women of the era, the Japanese garden—standing in for Japanese culture—was a powerful symbol of feminine refinement. The Gotō family, who maintained the garden, dressed in kimonos when the Huntingtons entertained.

The wisteria arbor,
a feature common to Japanese stroll gardens,
frames a view of a drum bridge for visitors
just after they pass through
the main gate.

The original Japanese Garden (overleaf),
on the site of a former small reservoir,
was chosen because Asian plant species
could survive the cold draughts
at the canyon's bottom.

The Bonsai Court (above),
hidden from the adjacent
Zen-style Garden by a "spirit screen,"
hosts trees from the
collection of the Huntington and
the Golden State Bonsai Federation.

The Zen-style garden (right),
built in 1967
by Robert Watson
and two Japanese assistants,
mimics the Honbō garden
at Daitokuji, Kyoto.

In the late 1950s, when the house, collections, and gardens were opened to the public, talk of tearing down the Japanese gardens was silenced when the San Marino Guild—a local women's group—exerted its influence to preserve the garden. In the next decades, decaying older structures such as the torii gate (erected for Huntington), fence, and thatched pavilion were destroyed even as new ornaments were added and paths built. (In recent years, disability legislation has forced further changes in the paths.) The Guild, devoted to ikebana flower arrangement, even erected an ikebana house alongside the garden. The most dramatic change occurred in 1965 when Japanese garden curator Robert Watson proposed a Zen-style rock garden to be built on a hillside south of the Japanese house. In contrast to the quaint beauty displayed by the red arched bridge and meandering paths of the 1912 garden, the "Zen garden" paralleled the postwar sense of Japanese culture that associated abstract minimalism with Zen aesthetics. Where in 1962 the Brooklyn Botanic Garden replicated the famous Ryōanji Garden, Watson used photos to adapt the rectangular arrangement of stone, raked gravel, and small shrubs in front of a tile-covered wall from the lesser-known Honbō Garden at Daitokuji in Kyoto. Completed in 1968 with the assistance of Eiichi Nunokawa and Sueo Serisawa, the garden opens south onto a bonsai court and is approached from the north by a dramatic bridge and a short flight of stairs.

The Huntington Japanese Gardens—backdrop for countless films and television shows set in Japan—offer a capsule history of twentieth-century Japanese-style gardens in the west, where formal features originally designed for Buddhist temples or the residences of samurai and aristocratic elite are pressed into a variety of new purposes: Marsh's original commercial garden, meant to lure consumers who would buy souvenirs, became a status symbol for a wealthy couple seeking to polish their cultural pedigree; fifty years later an institution similarly conscious of maintaining cultural prominence constructed a "Zen garden" and, more recently, removed the exoticizing red paint from the drum bridge. For the twenty-first century, the Huntington plans the addition of a teahouse and one of the world's largest Chinese gardens—a nod to the growing economic and cultural power of the area's Chinese population.

The Japanese house (left), first constructed in 1903 for G. T. Marsh's Japanese Tea Garden in Pasadena, was relocated to the Huntington estate in 1912.

The zigzag bridge (below) marks a transition from the Japanese house to the Zen-style garden.

The arched drum bridge (overleaf), built for the Huntingtons by Tōichirō Kawai ca. 1913, was originally painted red, as was a nearby torii gate.

Hakone Gardens

Saratoga, California

Among the millions of visitors who viewed the Japanese pavilions and garden at the 1915 Panama-Pacific International Exposition in San Francisco, perhaps none was more impressed than Isabel Longdon Stine (1880–1959). She visited often, drawn to the tea ceremony exhibitions sponsored by the Japan Central Tea Association. Stine's devotion to Japan and to music—she helped found the San Francisco Opera Company—led her to spend six months in Tokyo studying kabuki in 1917. Soon after the death of her husband, San Francisco real estate tycoon Oliver Charles Stine (1877–1918), she contracted carpenter Tsunematsu Shintani (1877–1921) to construct a pavilion and *shoin*-style Japanese house on the Moon-Viewing Hill of her recently purchased estate in Saratoga, nestled in the Santa Cruz mountains above the Santa Clara Valley. In this house, furnished with *tokonoma* alcove, tatami mats, and lavishly painted sliding-door panels, Stine and her children spent weekends and summers, sleeping on futons and using only Japanese furnishings except for a piano. In 1919 she hired Naoharu Aihara (1870–1940), a Palo Alto tailor formerly employed in the Golden Gate Park Japanese Tea Garden, to build a pond-style stroll garden. The garden features a pond, fed by a three-part waterfall, with a central island connected to the northern shore by an arched bridge. The Moon-Viewing Hill behind it was originally planted with cherries. In 1922 Shintani was called upon to design a teahouse and a second house in the flat area near the pond. Although Japanese on the exterior, the house had a bungalow-like interior more conducive to Western furnishings. A kabuki-style gate marked the entry to the entire compound—which Stine called Hakone after the scenic area near Mt. Fuji.

In many ways the Hakone garden complex was a theatrical stage set for Isabel Stine's converging interests in Japan and musical drama. She sometimes dressed her children, and their neighbor friends Joan Fontaine and Olivia de Haviland, in Japanese costume. In 1923 Hakone hosted an informal performance by the San Francisco Opera of Puccini's *Madama Butterfly*. Stine played the character of

The wisteria arbor (above)
overlooking the pond was a favorite spot
for the original owner's tea parties.

Rustic wooden wells (left)
were a favorite picturesque element
at many nineteenth-century Japanese gardens as
well as at the first Japanese-style gardens built in
North America.

the American wife. The garden also served as the backdrop for Stine's 1924 marriage to Francis W. Leis, and was the venue for such Japanese cultural events as a 1928 archery demonstration. In 1931 Stine rented the property to the Japanese consul-general and in 1932, after being hard hit in the Depression, she sold the sixteen-acre estate to financier Charles C. Tilden (1858–1950). His gardener James Sasaki made several changes to the garden, often counseled by Aihara. In 1940–41 local carpenter Shinzaburō Nishiura and several assistants rebuilt the arched bridge and constructed an impressive entry gate. After the property was sold in 1960, the new owners erected a torii-style gate at the base of the driveway.

When the property was offered in 1966, the Saratoga City Council purchased it as a city park, and hired Kyoto-trained Tanso Ishihara as caretaker in 1968. The enterprising Ishihara formed the Hakone Gardens Japanese Cultural Society in 1970, published a book on the garden in 1974, and planned restoration of the architecture and a dry garden in front of the Lower House, which was finished in 1981, one year after Ishihara's death. Ishihara introduced to Hakone his friend Kiyoshi Yasui, a garden designer, construction company owner, and Rotarian from Mukō-shi, a small town on the edge of Kyoto. Yasui helped Saratoga set up a sister-city arrangement with Mukō and encouraged the new Hakone Foundation to expand the garden by constructing in 1987 the Bamboo Park Kizuna-en (maintained by the Japan Bamboo Society of Saratoga) and in 1991 the Cultural Exchange Center, a full-size repro-duction of a nineteenth-century Kyoto merchant's house and shop. Featuring a tea ceremony room, tea "museum," studios for Japanese crafts, and Japanese-style apartments for artists in residence, the center was funded by a private donation from Japan to match $400,000 raised by the Hakone Foundation (but in fact loaned by the city of Saratoga). The tension between the foundation's plans for expansion coupled with cultural programs and their financial difficulties recalls Isabel Stine's own grand dreams and eventual difficulties. In a striking parallel to Stine, the foundation uses Hakone for tea ceremonies, tours, annual moon-viewing events, weddings, and performances by artists and musicians seeking to bridge Japan and America.

The Bamboo Park Kizuna-en (right), built at Hakone in 1987, features many varieties of bamboo as well as a dry garden with five large stones representing the five members of the Saratoga City Council.

The Upper House on the Moon-Viewing Hill (overleaf) was constructed by Tsunematsu Shintani in 1922 as a Japanese-style residence for the owner.

Kubota Garden

Seattle, Washington

Despite the many Japanese-style gardens in North America, only a few large gardens have been built for Japanese Americans or Japanese Canadians. One example is the Kubota Garden in Seattle, which evolved from a private family retreat into a commercial nursery and then a public park. Many Japanese emigrated to the west coast of North America between 1900 and 1920, settling in cities and rural areas of California, Oregon, Washington, and British Columbia. In the 1930s many of these first generation Japanese immigrants had decided to settle permanently in their adopted country though barred from becoming citizens or directly owning land. A few of these issei possessed both the money and desire to build Japanese-style gardens to remind them of their homeland, stand as a symbol of their success, and serve as a focus for the community. While most gardens—such as those in California for Unosuke Higashi in Monterey, Zenjūrō Shibata in Mt. Eden, T. Fukunaga in Los Angeles, and Kiyoshi Hirasaki in Gilroy, and in Washington for Chiyokichi Natsuhara in Auburn, and Kuni Mukai on Vashon Island—have been destroyed or are still private, Fujitarō Kubota's garden alone stand as public testament to a Japanese American who built "American Japanese" gardens.

Kubota (1880–1973), born and raised in Japan's Kōchi Prefecture, came to America around 1906, settling in Seattle were he worked first at a sawmill, then on a farm and in a hotel before establishing the Kubota Gardening Company in 1923. By 1929 the business had prospered to the extent that Kubota bought twenty acres in the Rainier Beach area of south Seattle. Deciding to create an authentic garden, Kubota researched landscapes in Japan, where he was most impressed by the stunning ponds and pine-flanked paths at Ritsurin Park in Takamatsu. Kubota, working with his sons Tom and Tak as well as with friends, first created a small waterfall-fed pond garden, featuring a stone bridge and lantern, and planted with iris, maples, and pines. Kubota next rechanneled Mapes Creek to feed a "necklace of ponds," the largest spanned by two stone bridges; a vermilion "heart bridge" carries

*Bridges of cut granite
and vermilion-painted wood span
the "necklace of ponds,"
built when Fujitarō Kubota decided to expand his
garden early in the 1930s.*

a road between two of the ponds. Kubota's garden and the large surrounding lawns served as a favorite spot for annual, summer *bon* dances and picnics with other immigrants from Kōchi. These activities were brought to a sudden halt after Pearl Harbor with the internment of Kubota and other "persons of Japanese descent" living in the coastal regions of the Pacific states and provinces. The Kubotas, except for the eldest son, Tom, who was drafted, spent the four war years at the Minidoka Camp in western Idaho, where Fujitarō utilized his talent as head of the garden detail.

Returning to Seattle after the war, Kubota rebuilt his landscaping business, eventually creating Japanese-style gardens at residences (including the future Bloedel Reserve) and at Seattle University. He also refurbished his abandoned property, building a large "drive-through" nursery or "automobile stroll garden" in which clients could motor through the lavishly planted grounds, choosing plant specimens or design ideas to take back to their own gardens. Kubota's integration of Japanese garden features with American function was further expressed in the Mountainside Garden, built early in the 1960s. More than four hundred tons of stone were relocated to create a series of paths that wind past two waterfalls, along a creek, to a memorial stone, and finally to a lookout. Where the other gardens on the property primarily utilize Japanese plants, here species native to the Pacific Northwest predominate. The garden synthesizes effects from Japan with the scenery of the Cascades. In 1972, the year before his death, the Japanese government awarded

The mix of plants native to Japan and to the Pacific Northwest help create this self-consciously "American Japanese garden."

Kubota the Fifth Class Order of the Sacred Treasure in recognition of "his achievements in his adopted country, for introducing and building respect for Japanese Gardening in this area."

When the Kubota property was eyed by developers, community organizations urged the Seattle Landmarks Preservation Board to save the core land. Designated a historical landmark by the city of Seattle in 1981 and acquired by the city in 1987, the Kubota house and garden are maintained by the Department of Parks and Recreation. The nonprofit Kubota Garden Foundation, established in 1989, promotes, preserves, and protects the garden by raising funds, offering tours, and holding workshops. This garden testifies to the adaptability of Japanese people—and Japanese-style gardens—in strange lands.

Rhododendrons (overleaf) highlight the lush planting, which discloses the original function of the Kubota Garden as a nursery.

The Bloedel Reserve
Bainbridge Island, Washington

The number and variety of Japanese-style gardens outside Japan testifies to the adaptability of the various Japanese landscape styles. Japanese garden design has prospered in the very different prewar and postwar aesthetic climates. Moreover, Japanese-style gardens have been built in large areas around ponds and in small areas without water. The remarkable fluidity of this genre is evident in two entirely different gardens inspired by Japanese design at the Bloedel Reserve—gardens which despite their massive formal differences were built in order to synthesize the admiration of nature central to Asian garden design with contemporary Western ideas about landscape.

When the University of Washington Arboretum erected its Japanese garden in 1960, Prentice and Virginia Bloedel were among the many persons in the Seattle area to contribute to this project and to be influenced by it. In 1961 Prentice Bloedel, a lumber industry magnate, hired garden builder Fujitarō Kubota to construct a garden at the Middle Pond at his 160-acre estate amidst the rainforests and meadows of Bainbridge Island. Kubota blocked off the end of the large pond to construct a much smaller body of water tucked against a forested hillside on the southwest and south, and flanked by gravel strolling paths on the northwest and east. Kubota directed the placement of large stones along the shoreline and the planting of Japanese red, black, and white pines, lace-leaf maple, cypress, juniper, cedar, yew, and bamboo from his large nursery in south Seattle. While many of the trees were pruned in the classical "cloud" and "boat" styles, the garden was conspicuous in its lack of such Japanese ornaments as bridges, lanterns, and shrines. While Kubota was building the garden, Bloedel engaged Paul Hayden Kirk of Seattle to construct a guest house blending elements of modernism, Japanese design, and the Native American longhouse. Kirk also designed a torii-style gate west of the structure and suggested that earthen mounds replace the oriental-style wooden face separating the swimming pool north of the house from the broad meadow beyond it. In the late 1970s, after Kubota died, Richard Yamasaki was hired to make improvements on Kubota's garden. Yoshirō Watanabe also designed and installed a stone path and string-tied fence connecting the guest house with the driveway.

The formal stone path,
designed by Yoshirō Watanabe in 1961,
leads from the driveway
to the Guest House.

In 1978 Bloedel employed well-known landscape architect Richard Haag to design several new gardens. Haag, who had spent two years at Kyoto University on a Fulbright Fellowship in the mid-1950s, created the Garden of Planes, or "Buddhist Garden of Mindfulness," in the area formerly occupied by the pool adjacent to the guest house. It was composed of a "rectangle of two nuanced, but unequal, pyramids" above a "horizontal plane of checked square stones and moss," but Bloedel, and those who took control of the garden after his death, felt the design was too artificial and removed it. Kōichi Kawana, a Southern California garden designer noted for his large stroll gardens, was hired in 1986 as a subcontractor for the Japanese garden. He created a raked sand and rock garden in the old pool—adapting Mirei Shigemori's famous 1939 garden at Tōfukuji—as well as a nearby moss and stone garden traversed by stepping stones brought from Bouquet Canyon near Los Angeles.

The creation of the Japanese gardens on the site constituted an important theoretical step for the Bloedel Reserve. Bloedel had written in 1977 of his respect for trees and the "divine order" of nature of which man is part. As such, the reserve had "much in common with gardens of the Orient." Thus, "we would like to capture the essence of the Japanese garden—the qualities of naturalness, subtlety, reverence, tranquillity—and construct a Western expression of it." The idea that landscape should "inspire and refresh the human spirit"—in the words of Reserve Director Richard Brown—is a direct outgrowth of Bloedel's sympathy for Japanese garden design and theory. In terms of the historical construction of the reserve, the 1960 garden was the first of what would become a half-dozen different landscape vignettes. Because of the Japanese or "Japanesque" appearance and philosophy of the reserve, it has hosted occasional ikebana flower arranging groups and haiku poetry readings.

The Middle Pond (above) was designed by Fujitarō Kubota to synthesize Japanese garden features with the native rain forest.

The small gate designed by Paul Kirk (right) marks the transition from the formal garden at the Guest House to the informal garden of the Middle Pond.

*Kōichi Kawana's garden of 1986,
in and around the former swimming pool of the guest house,
replaced landscape architect Richard's Haag's
abstract 1978 Garden of Planes,
adapting or parodying the stone garden at Tōfukuji.*

The UCLA Hannah Carter Japanese Garden
Los Angeles, California

*The garden,
originally built by
oil magnate Gordon Guiberson
and his wife,
is filled with souvenirs
of their trips to Japan.*

The status of most Japanese-style gardens in North America derives from the ability of their patrons to pose them as substitutes for gardens in Japan. As a simulacrum of the generic "Japanese garden," the garden on foreign soil fulfills the functions of serenity and purity attributed to historical gardens in Japan. As such it demonstrates the patron's status based on the level of his or her esoteric knowledge and heightened aesthetic appreciation. Any lien on authenticity must be demonstrated in the physical construction of the garden—usually by utilizing real Japanese materials and workers and copying features from well-known Japanese gardens—and in its ideological construction, manifest in the texts written about it. The UCLA Hannah Carter Japanese Garden demonstrates both claims in its construction and in the booklets published first by its original owner and then by its current steward, the University of California, Los Angeles.

On the hill behind his home in the fashionable Bel Air section of Los Angeles, from 1959 to 1961 oil-man Gordon Guiberson built a Japanese-style garden, naming it Shikyōen, or "Garden That Reminds One of Kyoto." Manifesting Guiberson's long interest in Japanese art, it was dedicated to his late mother Ethel Guiberson, a garden enthusiast. Guiberson and his wife had traveled to Japan twice, falling in love with the beauty of gardens in Kyoto; they then studied Japanese-style gardens in America. To design their garden they hired Nagao Sakurai, a noted Japanese designer who planned the 1939 Japanese gardens for San Francisco's Golden Gate International Exposition and for the New York World's Fair, and who had immigrated to California in 1953. For the Guiberson garden, Sakurai sought to adapt features of Kyoto gardens admired by the Guibersons to the hillside setting and preexisting Spanish-style garden, built in 1927 by A. E. Hansen for Harry Calandar. In 1965 Edward Carter, department store magnate and regent of the University of California, bought the property and gave the garden to UCLA to honor his wife, Hannah.

The garden is entered from the bottom by a stone-based stucco and tile gate copied from a gate at the Ichida estate in Kyoto's Nanzenji district. Built by Yoichirō Yoshihara in Japan, it was dismantled, shipped to Los Angeles, and reassembled by Kazuo Nakamura. A Katsura-style bamboo fence extends from the gate. Inside, stone steps pass imported water basins and a stone with fifteen carved images of Buddha. The garden contains nearly a thousand tons of stone from Santa Paula Canyon in Ventura County and quarries near Mt. Baldy, but the most important stones, along with the numerous water basins, lanterns, and other ornaments, were brought from Japan. The flat, lower section of the garden features a koi pond encrusted with plants, small lanterns, a stone pagoda, a black pebble beach, and stones including the flat "thinking stone" as well as the 9.5-ton "boat stone." The intimate pond, fed by a dramatic waterfall, is crossed in one corner by a low bridge and at its center by two rectangular paving stones and three circular mill stones—an adaptation of stones at the pond garden of Heian Jingū. A rusticated, shingled teahouse overlooks the pond. The teahouse also seems to float above a "river" of smooth white pebbles flowing from the hill above. Several steep paths ascend the heavily planted hillside to converge on the "Hokora shrine." Made by the Kyoto artisans who built the entry gate, this small cryptomeria-roofed structure houses a gilt wooden Buddha. The east part of the hill contains three functional areas: at top is a stone bathhouse, left over from the Spanish garden, with a sunken bath fed by a rivulet; in the middle is an open wooden deck for "moon viewing" with a Japanese-railing featuring *giboshi*; at bottom is a barbecue area with a stone counter designed by Nakamura. The extreme western part of the garden features a spectacular "Hawaiian waterfall."

Despite the obvious inauthenticities of the Hawaiian cataract, patio deck, barbecue terrace, Spanish-style bathhouse, and numerous live oaks, as well as the crowded pastiche of the Japanese elements, Guiberson's original booklet and UCLA's subsequent pamphlet present the garden as virtually authentic. Both begin with histories of Japanese gardens and then discuss the "principal features within the garden" in terms of their relation to Japanese garden history, asserting that this garden could just as well have been made in mid-seventeenth-century Kyoto as in mid-twentieth-century Los Angeles. For its owners, the pleasure and status derived from the garden stem from these claims of authenticity and, by extension, legitimacy.

The small, flat area at the base of this hillside garden is filled with a thousand tons of California stone, and other "important" stones brought from Japan.

The entry path
at the bottom of the garden (left) is
composed of tons of
local stone as well as Japanese water
basins and a stone carved with sixteen
Buddha images (above).

*Although named
"Garden That Reminds
One of Kyoto,"
its arrangement
on a steep hill
and the presence of
California live oaks
lend a
Southern Californian
ambiance.*

Ganna Walska Lotusland Japanese Garden
Montecito, California

Most large Japanese-style gardens on estates were built in the first decades of the twentieth century when the Gilded Age expressed itself in part through opulent collections of exotic gardens. However, postwar elites have also built large Japanese gardens as spaces for escape and as a way of expressing their economic might and cultural sophistication. While in the 1960s Avery Brundage and Barbara Hutton built rock gardens resembling Ryōanji, and in the 1990s Lawrence Ellison and John Kluge constructed gardens based on Katsura Villa and "Moss Temple" of Saihōji, Madame Ganna Walska pursued a unique vision on her estate Lotusland in the exclusive enclave of Montecito, California. Although Walska, a Polish diva whose fortune came from her former husbands (particularly the industrialist Alexander Smith Cochran), had never been to Japan, the popularity of Japanese-style gardens among such friends as Barbara Hutton and the exotic associations of the genre likely fueled her desire for one.

   In 1941 Walska bought the ninety-eight-acre estate Cuesta Linda, formerly known as Tanglewood and owned by nursery man Ralph Kinton Stevens. Walska's purchase was precipitated by Theos Bernard, the self-proclaimed "White Lama of Tibet," who would soon become Walska's sixth husband and who wanted to use the property as a retreat for Tibetan Buddhist monks. Walska named the property Tibetland. After the couple divorced in 1946, Walska turned her prodigious energy to her estate, renamed it Lotusland, and hired Ralph T. Stevens to design a theater garden, blue garden, and topiary garden—all additions to the earlier olive allée, lotus pond, water lily ponds, water stair, parterre, Moorish fountain, and formal gardens. Stevens may have been responsible for the distinctive cactus and succulent plant-ings. In 1967 Walska decided to turn a man-made "lake," used to grow lotus, into a pond at the center of a Japanese garden. After commissioning and rejecting designs from Eijirō Nunokawa and two other Los Angeles landscapers, she selected local stonemason Oswald da Ros and gardener Frank Fujii.

The dramatic bronze cranes and dozens of lanterns
reflect the theatrical taste of the original owner, Madame Ganna Walska,
a former opera diva.

Kawana's additions
to the garden (overleaf) include a rock beach,
recalling those of seventeenth-century
Japanese stroll gardens.

Da Ros and Fujii were intimately familiar with Walska's operatic taste, and with local gardens, having worked in many of them as teenagers with their fathers: Fujii was the son of Kinzuchi Fujii, the builder of many Japanese-style gardens in Santa Barbara and Ojai in the 1930s, and the lavish Storrier-Stearns garden in Pasadena in the late 1930s. Together the men trucked in tons of stone from the nearby San Marcos Pass and Dos Pueblos Ranch, but also went as far as Nipomo, Temecula, and Mt. Palomar for rock to line the pond, the stream which feeds it, and the strolling path around the pond. In addition to purchasing lanterns from various companies, da Ros and Fujii scoured the old estates where their fathers had built homes or gardens, buying or otherwise acquiring lanterns and related garden ornaments. The stone torii at one entrance to the garden came from a Santa Barbara residence, several lanterns were bought from Avery Brundage's nearby fire-ravaged house and stone garden, a snow-viewing lantern was acquired from the El Mirador estate, several more lanterns were saved from Lora Knight's garden (where Kinzuchi Fujii's 1930 teahouse had recently burned in a fire), and two formal lanterns came from a Santa Barbara bank. In many ways a stroll through this garden is a walk through the history of Montecito-area Japanese gardens from 1900 to 1965. The seventeen species of broadleaf trees, thirty species of conifers, two varieties of palms, cycads, twenty-eight shrub species, three types of bamboo, and six varieties of ferns provide a visual richness equaling that of the lanterns, water basins, and stone pagodas. Several bronze cranes placed in the pond complete the beautiful, exotic dreamland which characterizes Walska's vision of the entire complex of gardens at Lotusland.

After Walska's death in 1984, the Ganna Walska Lotusland Foundation took control of the garden and in 1986 commissioned Japanese-garden designer Kōichi Kawana to make modifications in order to create a more "authentic" Japanese garden. His chief additions were a wisteria arbor, built in 1991, and a small thatch-roofed Kasuga-style shrine (hokora) placed on a stone base between two large granite lanterns already on site. Walska's romantic and theatrical interest in the Japanese garden continues in fund-raisers held by the foundation. In July 1995 three hundred guests were invited to "Lotusland Celebrates Twilight With Madama Butterfly," complete with taiko drummer, Japanese tunes played on a flute, and arias from Puccini's Madame Butterfly.

This adaptation of a stone lantern
and a well-style water basin
from the tea ceremony garden
adds an intimate touch.
The wooden bridge demonstrates
the creative fusion of elements characteristic
of North American gardens.

Ganna Walska Lotusland Japanese Garden

Kawana's additions
to the garden
include a rock beach,
recalling those of
seventeenth-century
Japanese stroll gardens.

Washington Park Arboretum
Japanese Garden
Seattle, Washington

In the first decades of the twentieth century, the Japanese garden represented for westerners perhaps the most sophisticated and spiritually evolved type of landscape design. However, from the mid-1930s through the early 1950s political hostility toward Japan brought a twenty-year lull in widespread construction of Japanese-style gardens in North America. By the late 1950s the Japanese garden was once more in fashion, featured in books and magazine articles, contrived in suburban yards, and discussed by civic boards. The Japanese Garden at the Washington Park Arboretum in Seattle represents the earliest postwar public construction of a Japanese-style garden on the Pacific Coast and, as such, had a great impact on other gardens, serving as the template in design and function for most of the large civic pond-and-teahouse gardens built over the next forty years.

In 1937 the officers of the newly created Arboretum Foundation in Washington Park invited Japan's International Cultural Society (Kokusai Bunka Shinkōkai) to create a five-acre Japanese garden on Foster Island. War tension soon led both sides to terminate the plan. Twenty years later Mrs. Neil Haig of the Arboretum Foundation Special Projects Committee proposed revisiting the old plan for a Japanese Garden—an idea brought to fruition by an anonymous gift from logging magnate and garden devotee Prentice Bloedel. Asked by the foundation to recommend a designer, the Japanese consul general in Seattle contacted the Ministry of Foreign Affairs which in turn asked Tokyo city officials who chose Jūki Iida (1889–1977). Iida, working with plans drawn up in Japan by master designer Shin Idoshita and modified by Iida and five associates, came to Seattle in fall 1959 to investigate the three-and-a-half-acre site before beginning what he thought was to be four years' construction. Seattle officials, however, urged Iida to build the garden immediately, so he chose second-generation Japanese American Kei Ishimitsu as architecture specialist, William Yorozu as plant manager, and Dick Yamasaki as stone

The north end of the garden pond features the geometric "fishing village," its sharp lines a dramatic contrast with the rounded azaleas (above) and drooping wisteria (overleaf).

91

manager (Iida and Yamasaki gathered more than five hundred granite stones from the banks of Snoqualmie River). Iida oversaw the placement of rocks, the setting of stone lanterns, and the planting of native pines, firs, maples, and shrubs—even acquiescing to local requests to utilize the "gaudy" rhododendron. The garden opened June 5, 1960, with free admission for anyone wearing a kimono.

A formal-style, pond-type stroll garden, it features paths circling a large pond fed at the south by two streams which descend a hillside. From the entry gate a path leads north through a densely planted grove and then forks, the eastern path skirting the pond and leading past a spit of land covered with beach stones and capped with a small lantern. The center of the pond contains a small "tortoise island" planted with pines and reached by a plank bridge from the west and earthen bridge from the east—the direction of the small Emperor's Gate. In the northeastern part of the garden a wisteria trellis marks a transition to the dramatically geometric "fishing village," with its cut-stone "boat dock" and formal path turning at right angles to parallel the rectilinear edge of the pond. The path then curves south, passing the *azumaya* (viewing arbor) on a low hill, then the moon-viewing stand perched on the shoreline. Southeast of the pond is the tea garden enclosing the *machiai* (waiting arbor) and teahouse—originally gifts from the people of Tokyo. When the teahouse burned in 1973, it was rebuilt with funds raised by local groups as well as the Urasenke Foundation of Japan, the largest of Japan's tea ceremony organiza-

The small "tortoise island" in the center of pond (below), symbolic of longevity, is reached from the east by a zigzag bridge (right).

tions. Renamed Shōseian (Arbor of Murmuring Pines), it is used for classes by the
Seattle Urasenke chapter and for monthly public demonstrations from April through
October. The entire garden features ten lanterns, including, on the "mountainside" at
its north end, a three-and-a-half-ton lantern donated by Seattle's sister city, Kōbe.
The garden was administrated by the University of Washington until 1981 when
management and operation were transferred to the Seattle Department of Parks and
Recreation. The nonprofit Japanese Garden Society helps fund and maintain the
garden, hosting classes in garden history and maintenance, school tours, and
special events including a moon-viewing ceremony. The garden also serves as a
living laboratory for several courses at the nearby University of Washington. In its
large scale, multifaceted design, community activities, and self-promotion as "the
next best thing to being in Japan," the style, function, and ideology of the garden
have been much imitated but rarely matched.

The elegant Shōseien Teahouse (left)
occupies a low hill in the
informal southern portion of the garden.

Seen from the hill at its north end,
the geometry of the near shoreline (below)
sets off the elegant curves
characteristic of most of the pond.

Nitobe Memorial Garden

Vancouver, British Columbia

Japanese-style gardens in North America often serve a variety of functions unrelated to those of gardens in Japan, which they claim to mimic both formally and philosophically. Moreover, despite rhetoric that these gardens provide an allegory for life or embody other heady spiritual concepts, public gardens fulfill the immediate political and social goals of their patrons. The Nitobe Memorial Garden at the University of British Columbia commemorates the university's orientation toward Asia and, more specifically, Japan-Canada relations; it cements ties with the local Japanese Canadian community; it is deployed by culture groups such as the Urasenke tea ceremony organization; it provides a place for students and faculty to study Japanese culture and botany; and finally, it is rented for weddings and other social activities.

On October 15, 1933, Dr. Inazō Nitobe, a member of the Japanese House of Peers and undersecretary general of the League of Nations, was on his way to a peace conference when he suddenly died in Vancouver. To commemorate the famous Japanese pacifist, his friends in western Canada and at the University of British Columbia built a small Japanese-style garden with a lantern on the west side of the campus. The garden was vandalized during World War II, allowed to deteriorate further in the 1950s, and finally destroyed by the construction of a dormitory in 1959. A university committee—composed of faculty, a Japanese Canadian community representative, and the Japanese consul—proposed a large new garden, with its "authenticity" guaranteed by a Japanese designer, to express the university's commitment to the local Japanese community and to international goodwill. Money, raised from the Canada Council, Leon and Thea Korner Foundations, Japan-Canada Society in Tokyo, and various Japanese Canadian organizations in British Columbia, was used to purchase materials, while the university contributed a 2.2-acre site in the northwest corner of the campus. The committee asked the Japanese consul in Vancouver to consult his government concerning a designer, and the Foreign Ministry chose Kannosuke Mori of Chiba University. Mori spent many months in Vancouver laying out the garden and placing the stones and plants. The garden was dedicated in June 1960.

A stream descending along an artificial hill feeds the pond at the garden's center.

*A flat wooden bridge
and gently bowed earthen bridge add
visual interest to the undulating
shoreline of the pond-style stroll garden.*

The various shades of green
recall the monochromatic quality of such Japanese
gardens as Saihōji in Kyoto.

The stroll garden's paths lead around and over a large, elongated pond filled with carp brought in 1964. The pond is fed by a stream and a waterfall located on an artificial hill in the east corner of the garden. From the entrance gate a path leads around a low hillock and opens onto a view of the relocated Nitobe Memorial Lantern (one of twelve lanterns in the garden) and a large island reached by a wooden bridge. The sides of the pond are dotted with local stones and the waterfall uses colorful rocks from nearby Harrison Lake. Two granite slabs, placed side by side, cross the stream near the waterfall. At its narrow waist the pond is bisected by a large earthen bridge composed of a timber frame overlaid with bundles of brushwood and covered with compacted earth. A seven-tiered stone pagoda and a rustic viewing pavilion stand at either edge of the bridge. In the pond's southern shallows a three-section zigzag bridge cuts through a bed of iris. The area from the paths to the garden's perimeter wall are covered with turf meant to replicate the texture of the zoysia found in Tokyo stroll gardens. Rows of huge hemlock and laurel screen the garden from the road outside and dampen the sound of the automobiles. South of the entrance is a fenced-in tea garden, utilizing stones procured at Britannia Beach, surrounding a teahouse constructed in Japan and then reassembled on-site.

On the southern shore of the pond,
the Ichibō'an Teahouse sits in its own enclosed garden.

Dedicated to statesman Inazō Nitobe, the Kasuga-style Nitobe Memorial Lantern stands sentinel just inside the garden's entry gate.

In 1992 the Nitobe Garden, now part of a campus "culture zone" composed of the Asia Centre, Museum of Anthropology, and First Nations' Longhouse, was designated for a $1.5 million restoration funded largely by the Japanese Business Association of Vancouver, various Japanese corporations, the Japan Foundation, and the Commemorative Association of the 1970 Japan World Exposition. Overseen by Toshiaki Masuno of Japan Landscape Consultants in Yokohama, the bulk of the rebuilding was carried out by a team from Kyoto led by Shin'ichi Sano, an eighteenth-generation garden builder. In addition to the pruning and replacing of plants, the pond's shoreline was upgraded with one hundred tons of stone from Whistler and Squamish, several pebble beaches were added, a garden wall (*tsujibei*) and new entry were constructed, and the Urasenke Foundation donated funds for renovation of the Ichibō'an teahouse for use by the group's Vancouver chapter. In 1994 the university hosted an international symposium to commemorate the restoration of what they had termed a "*Japanese* Japanese garden in Canada."

*The intimate, hillside Natural Garden
of 1968, originally designed by
Takuma Tono as the Moss Garden,
was likely inspired by
Kyoto's famous Saihōji.*

The Japanese Garden
Portland, Oregon

Of the many public Japanese-style gardens in North America, the garden in Portland is often considered the most authentic and the most beautiful. While claims of its "authenticity" pose problems, the Portland garden doubtless offers the greatest variety of garden styles designed and maintained at the highest level. Just as the Washington Park Arboretum in Seattle and the University of British Columbia were launching gardens, and as the Brooklyn Botanic Garden was adding a copy of the stone garden at Ryōanji in Kyoto, a group of dedicated Portland citizens decided to create a garden unparalleled in scale, cost, and design. The most revolutionary aspect of the garden, however, is the plan incorporating five distinct Japanese garden styles into a single "Japanese garden."

Seeking ways to strengthen ties between Portland and Japan, the Japan Society of Oregon in 1959 proposed a sister city relationship and a garden for a commemorative teahouse, forming the Garden Committee. By 1962 the city-appointed Japanese Garden Commission (later the Japanese Garden Society of Oregon)—composed of members from the mayor's office, city council, garden clubs, Japanese Ancestral Society, Japanese Consulate and Japan Society—agreed to locate the garden in the 5.5-acre space of the old Washington Park Zoo above the International Rose Test Gardens. In 1963 they hired designer Takuma Tono (1891–1987), a professor at Tokyo Agricultural College with degrees from Hokkaidō University and Cornell University. In the 1920s Tono built gardens for Herbert Dow in Midland, Michigan, and in 1962 completed the Ryōanji replica in Brooklyn. With a $450,000 budget and city work crews, Tono laid out the rudiments of the Portland garden during trips between 1963 to 1965. To complete the garden, in 1966 he brought to Portland Kinya Washio, the first of eight "landscape directors" from Japan. Although the city of Portland pledged to use no tax money directly for the garden, substantial funds were allocated through the Park Bureau, whose workers did much basic construction. Many of the materials were donated by individuals, organizations, and corporations from both sides of the Pacific, making the Portland garden a "friendship garden" in fact if not in name.

An unusual square water basin (above) in the Natural Garden is one of more than three dozen carefully placed stone ornaments.

A stairway and paved path (left), utilizing stones recycled from Portland's former Civic Auditorium, lead to the rest shelter in the lowest corner of the Natural Garden.

Tono planned four distinct gardens: the Flat Garden just inside the entry gate, the Tea Garden, the Strolling Pond Garden, and the Sand and Stone Garden. The Flat Garden (*hiraniwa*), a sea of raked white sand surrounded by evergreens and azaleas and bearing the felicitous design of a gourd and sake cup composed of low groundcover, is best viewed from the west verandah of the pavilion constructed in 1980 by Skidmore, Owings & Merrill. Built of Alaskan cedar and roofed with Gifu tile, the pavilion adapts traditional Japanese architecture. Its east deck offers spectacular views of Portland and Mt. Hood—Oregon's Mt. Fuji. (The small, recently completed Viewpoint Garden, in front of the east deck, is used for annual moon-viewing events.) At the western edge of the entire complex is the monochromatic Tea Garden (*roji*), including an entry gate, waiting arbor (*machiai*), and the Kashintei (Flower Heart Pavilion) teahouse, which was designed by Tono, constructed in Japan, and reassembled in Portland in 1968. Because the Tea Garden is closed to the public, in 1984 an outer *roji* with *machiai* and gate was built northwest of the teahouse.

East of the spare Tea Garden is the dramatic Strolling Pond Garden (*chisen kaiyū-shiki*). From the undulating, rock-lined upper pond, spanned at its outlet by the graceful "moon bridge," a stream lined by hundreds of shrubs and several varieties of maples gently drops into an iris marsh traversed by a wood-planked zigzag bridge. The stream then flows into the koi-filled lower pond—the old zoo's bear pit—punctuated from below by dramatic stones and from above by Heavenly Falls cascading off a steep cliff. The twenty tons of stone lining the stream and ponds were brought

The zigzag bridge designed by Hachirō Sakakibara crosses an iris marsh, reprising a feature ubiquitous to Edo-period Japanese stroll gardens and large Japanese-style gardens in North America.

from the Columbia River Gorge. From the lower pond a path leads east down a steep hill through the intimate Natural Garden, originally called the Moss Garden when it opened in 1968. Here, two paths composed of various materials—including granite from the steps of the old Civic Auditorium—traverse a thickly forested hillside planted with azaleas, pines, and other shrubs, and bisected by a burbling stream. In the lowest area a rustic gate introduces a small, tile-roofed rest pavilion. From it a steep flight of steps climbs an azalea-covered hillside.

Perched halfway up the hill leading from the Natural Garden to the pavilion east of the Flat Garden is the dramatic, Zen-inspired Sand and Stone Garden (*sekitei*). Enclosed by a tile-topped stucco wall, this rectangular expanse of raked gravel is set with seven small stones "facing" a large vertical stone near the center of the enclosure. Garden pamphlets explain that the small stones represent seven tiger cubs swimming in the sea, while the large stone symbolizes the compassionate Buddha who saved them. In 1994 the stones were surrounded with moss-covered berms like those at the famous rock garden of Ryōanji. Much of the impact of the Portland garden derives from its impressive site and approach. From the parking area visitors can take a shuttle bus to the garden entrance or ascend a winding

A wisteria arbor frames the five-tier stone pagoda, presented by Portland's sister city, Sapporo, and placed in front of stones arranged in the shape of the island of Hokkaidō.

The verandah of the pavilion (left)
overlooks the Flat Garden (above) where,
in the midst of the raked sand, groundcover forms
a gourd and a sake cup.

five-hundred-foot path from the Antique Gate built in 1976 and set in a tile-topped stucco wall constructed in 1991. The entry gate, called the Daimyō Gate because it resembles the large gates outside the residences of feudal lords or *daimyō*, was finished in 1966.

The success of the Japanese Garden in Portland stems largely from its similarity to the most successful gardens in Japan. Yet it does not so much resemble them formally or spiritually; rather, like them, it has been ruthlessly revised, with old plantings and even designs altered by new garden directors. For all the rhetoric of "authenticity" and "purity," the garden has evolved virtually from the moment Tono made his preliminary sketches. The fluidity of the garden is largely attributable to the devotion of Garden Society members who have not only realized that beauty is in the details and given generously for decades, but have also viewed it as a setting for education about Japan and as a canvas for change. At the same time, however, the Portland garden typifies the theory and design of many postwar, civic "Japanese gardens" in its Disneyesque amalgamation of different historical and functional garden types into a single "Japanese garden," which, in the words of one early pamphlet, allows the viewer to "enjoy the quiet beauty of Japan in Portland, Oregon."

In the dramatic
Sand and Stone Garden (overleaf)
the seven flat stones reportedly
symbolize tiger cubs
while the vertical stone represents
the Buddha,
who saved them from drowning.

Japanese Friendship Garden, Kelley Park
San Jose, California

Friendship or sister city gardens are among the most common postwar Japanese-style gardens in North America. Of the several dozen in the United States and Canada, one of the earliest and most representative is the Japanese Friendship Garden in San Jose's Kelley Park. The garden is a living symbol of Japanese American community pride, of postwar American paternalism (or, more accurately, maternalism) toward Japan, of Japan's desire to present its most congenial face toward America, and of changing Asian ethnicity and patterns of garden use in late-twentieth-century cities.

In 1958, the year after San Jose established a sister city affiliation with Okayama, members of the women's Pilot Club expressed a desire to build a Japanese garden. A Japanese garden committee led by Edna Anthony negotiated with city government and local groups, and hired landscape designer Nagao Sakurai to present three different plans. By 1959, the city of San Jose, eager to alter its image as a featureless suburb, decided to utilize six acres of Kelley Park to build "*the* outstanding Japanese Garden of America*,*" including a restaurant and a large stroll garden based on the famous Kōrakuen garden in Okayama. In 1960, city and community leaders—including the sister city group Pacific Neighbors—debated different design possibilities and land allocation after appropriating $50,000. In 1962, Hisaichi Harry Tsugawa, designer of the small Japanese garden at Oakland's Lake Merritt, was hired as design consultant. During the next year the Japanese American Citizens' League, San Jose Landscape Gardener's Association, Nisei Veterans of Foreign Wars, San Jose Buddhist Church, and San Jose Methodist Church raised money and in-kind donations of labor and plants. Companies, such as the A. L. Raisch Paving Company, which donated 1,200 tons of rock, volunteered money and services. Construction started in 1964, and most of the planting was carried out by 140 Japanese Americans in March 1965. The garden was dedicated on October 31, 1965, with politicians attending from San Jose and Okayama—which donated carp and a lantern. Edna Anthony came from her hospital bed, and died just four days after seeing her dream realized.

*A grove of cherry trees
flanks the east side of the Middle Pond,
screening the garden from
a nearby road.*

The symbolic tortoise island in the Lower Pond is clearly suggested by the tile-like stones, which represent a tortoise's shell.

The Friendship Garden adapts the spacious pond-and-hills design of Okayama's Kōrakuen, using four thousand lineal feet of paths to take viewers past twenty-two focal points arranged around three ponds with a total water surface of more than one acre. Of the original three thousand koi in the garden ponds, only a few remain. More than 450 trees, 650 shrubs, and several acres of lawn studded with stones convert the once bare earth into a verdant oasis. The upper garden, entered through a wooden gate surmounted by a tile roof, is composed of the *shinji-ike* (heart pond) with a picturesque drum bridge leading to a chain of pine-covered islands. The pond empties to the north into a meandering stream, crossed twice by a path and running past a grove of cherries, then descends to a second pond. A tall stone pagoda dramatically accentuates the far shore. Both ponds drain into waterfalls, which spill into either end of the gourd-shaped lower pond. The pond is bisected by a bridge. Each half contains a tortoise island, with stones indicating the head, flippers, and tail as well as flat stones mounded to suggest a humped carapace. At the north end of the pond a wooden-planked bridge (*yatsuhashi*) crosses a bed of iris in front of the large food-service pavilion, called the *chaya* (teahouse). The restaurant, dedicated on May 18, 1970, originally served a variety of foods, but now contains a shop selling Japanese toys and souvenirs. It is rented out for meetings and other events.

Like several other civic gardens, the Kelley Park garden offers docent tours for school groups and other organizations. More unique is a special ranger-led "haiku tour" in which visitors study the several haiku stones—rocks with plaques inscribed with brief poems—and are invited to write their own poems expressing their impressions of the garden. This attempt to create an ongoing Japanese reading (or writing) of the garden is outweighed by the normative use of the garden. As the suburban Japanese American community, so instrumental in the garden's construction, has become increasingly estranged from the urban garden, the space has come to serve as a gathering spot for the growing Chinese and Southeast Asian populations resident in the neighborhood. Even though the design features are Japanese, they have been appropriated as generically "Asian" by Chinese, Vietnamese, and Thais who have little connection with the historical garden styles of their own cultures.

The omnipresent arched bridge of Japanese-style gardens leads to the so-called Tea Ceremony Island in the Upper Pond.

Survivors of predatory
raccoons and herons, colorful koi are
virtually mandatory in Japanese-style
gardens with ponds.

San Mateo Japanese Garden
San Mateo, California

In the 1950s and 1960s Japanese American men were most conspicuous in west coast cities in the occupations of landscape gardeners and nurserymen. These men frequently contributed their labor and materials to the construction of civic gardens. In San Mateo a group of Japanese American gardeners not only constructed but planned a garden symbolic of their place in American society. From the garden's opening a Japan-born gardener has served as "curator," and Japanese American women have worked there during the summer season.

In the mid-1950s the San Mateo Gardeners' Association decided to build a small garden in front of some local civic building to demonstrate their art and to symbolize their commitment to American society in the wake of World War II and the relocation of many Japanese Americans to internment camps. Plans to place a garden at City Hall were discouraged when the group realized that local government offices had a history of moving. A 1963 sister city arrangement between San Mateo and Toyonaka galvanized the gardeners to form in February 1965 the Kōen Kai (support association) to raise materials, funds, and labor. It also persuaded the city to contribute one-and-a-half acres in Central Park. Under the leadership of Sanaye Ikeda and Tom Takayama, the scope of the garden was expanded in response to a flood of donations and the interest of local garden groups, Japanese American organizations, and the city government. Nagao Sakurai, noted Japanese landscape designer resident in Berkeley since 1953, was enlisted to plan the garden. Construction commenced on October 22, 1965, and the garden was dedicated on August 28, 1966.

Sakurai designed a pond-centered stroll garden. Entered through the main gate, a teahouse (dedicated in 1968) stands to the left, offering a commanding view of the north section of the koi-filled pond fed by a two-step waterfall. A low wooden bridge bisects the narrow center of the pond then leads to several paths, which wind through the densely planted and slightly sloping east shore. A two-ton, five-story stone pagoda—given by Toyonaka—stands sentinel near the head of a small stream. The broad main garden path curves past a rhododendron forest at the southern section of the pond. While the main path curves around the bottom of the pond, an offshoot crosses a curved wooden bridge leading to a central island connected to the far shore by a second bridge. The southwest side of the pond features an azalea grove and a small, rustic viewing pavilion reached by six stone steps. Four stone lanterns—in the *yukimi*, Oribe, Kasuga, and *takara* styles—perch along the shore of the pond, and a single *nekoashi-maru* lantern sits by the stream. While several live oaks provide dramatic backdrops from just outside the garden's surrounding wall, inside Sakurai planted an overabundance of Asian and Western trees including five species of maples, fourteen types of pines (including bristlecone), cryptomeria, gingko, apricot, plum, cherry, three types of cypress, Portuguese laurel, red horse chestnut, several varieties of magnolia, Formosa sweetgum, banana shrub, and five rare types of beech. The distinguishing feature of the garden is Sakurai's careful placement of over two hundred tons of stone from Santa Rosa County. Of special note are the huge, flat-topped "key" stone in front of the main gate, a similar stone on the north end, and the "tortoise-and-crane" rock grouping near the bridge in the south pond. Sakurai skillfully used stones to form a dramatically varied pond edge, strategically incorporating small redwood posts and broad beaches of smooth pebbles to create a range of different forms and textures. The garden has been well maintained by a series of skilled curators including Sadao Sugimoto, Mitsuo Umehara, and Isamu (Sam) Fukudome.

The Azumaya,
or viewing pavilion,
built with funds donated by
the Garden Study Club of
the San Francisco Peninsula,
is all but obscured by the dense plantings
of trees and shrubs
that characterize this
garden of the mid-1960s.

The patronage and function of the garden reveal some of the community groups crucial to the garden's construction and its bicultural orientation. The Azumaya, or viewing pavilion, was erected with $2,500 given by the Garden Study Club of the Peninsula, while the largest bridge was funded with $1,200 raised by the Hillsborough Garden Club. Built two years after the garden opened, the teahouse has long been staffed by young, kimono-clad Japanese American women who served tea and snacks during the summer months. It also hosted occasional *koto* recitals, ikebana arrangements, and tea ceremony demonstrations. These activities, apprehended within the beauty of the garden, underscore the garden's original role in presenting Japanese culture to the San Mateo community.

During summer months young Japanese American women wearing kimono serve tea in the teahouse (above).

Although Nagao Sakurai designed many private residential gardens on the San Francisco peninsula, the San Mateo garden (overleaf) is his only completed public garden (photo: John Kiely).

The pavilion and zigzag bridge,
glimpsed only after several minutes of walking,
are the focal points of the ridge-top garden.

Hayward Japanese Garden
Hayward, California

The ubiquity of Japanese-style gardens in Western cities is based in part on the adaptability of their styles and cultural associations. Where a dry stone garden may fit a small urban site, a pond lends itself to a waterside stroll garden. Similarly, the "Japaneseness" of Japanese-style gardens can symbolize a Japanese American organization or a sister city arrangement with a Japanese city, even as the relative naturalism may be deemed appropriate for gardens in natural settings. The Hayward Japanese Garden, constructed in 1980 by the city of Hayward and the Hayward Area Recreation and Park District alongside a senior center and theater complex, serves to bridge natural and man-made environments even as it signals the city's transpacific ties.

In the mid-1960s the citizens of Hayward decided that a park should be developed on the old Hayward High School Botanical Garden, resting on a ridge between the Castro Valley and San Leandro creeks. In 1967 the Hayward Area Recreation and Park District officially designated the area as a future park site and in 1972, with the city of Hayward, acquired more land for a total of almost six acres. In 1977 an 11,500-square-foot Senior Citizen Center was built, with the 15,996-square-foot Little Theater Complex erected to its north in 1979. Both structures were constructed in pseudo-Japanese styles with shingled, hipped-and-gabled roofs and walls faced with white stucco and wooden posts. In 1980 the 1.3-acre "Japanese Garden" was built on the southern tip of the promontory. Each of Hayward's community centers has a theme related to the culture of one sister city: Hayward's connection to Funabashi, Japan, is acknowledged here.

To build the Japanese Garden, the city and the Hayward Area Recreation and Park District galvanized support among the local Japanese American community, including the Hayward branch of the Japanese American Citizens' League as well as nursery and gardener groups. Kimio Kimura, a U.C. Berkeley–trained landscape architect resident in San Francisco, approached the District with design plans and was awarded the commission. The garden embodies Kimura's ideas on adapting the principles of Japanese landscape design to Western spaces and, specifically, to the California climate. Roughly seventeen Japanese plant types are mixed with several dozen Western species. Both trees and shrubs are carefully pruned and grouped with other species or with stones to express the "dynamic balance" central to Kimura's grammar of "rational organicism." Water, central in Kimura's system, is present both in its actual form and in several dry streams and waterfalls composed

The distinctive rock and plant forms characteristic of Kimio Kimura's concept of "occult balance" are best seen in the dry streams.

of gravel and stones that descend through the dense plantings. The arrangements are intended to suggest either fast or slow moving water. Although the garden is small, it seems larger due to the careful arrangement of over three thousand feet of paths, which wind through banks of plants and around a pond, with views of the garden structures hidden and then revealed. After passing through the entry gate, the main path—followed in a clockwise direction—leads past a covered waiting bench (overlooking San Leandro Creek below the garden), a pond pavilion, a teahouse, and finally an arbor. The four-thousand-square-foot pond is fed by a waterfall, banked by much of the eighty tons of field stone used in the garden and overlooked by a wooden observation pavilion. Raised above the water on six pillars, it references both Japanese tradition and California patio design. The pavilion looks south across the pond past a wooden bridge toward the "teahouse." Again the architectural form adapts Japanese design, specifically the *shinmei* style of Ise Shrine, to the casual materials of municipal park architecture. The garden also contains a rock sculpture donated by the city of Funabashi in 1994.

A pamphlet published for the garden's dedication observes that Japanese gardens teach that "through Nature, Man can gain the perspective necessary to bear his troubles easily, for in Nature are forces far more harsh and fearsome than those which mankind must deal with daily." The teaching accords with Kimura's belief that the Japanese garden provides a setting for spiritual enlightenment, a place of tranquillity, as well as a democratic space in which all parts are interdependent. In America this is not achieved by copying Japanese effects, but by the dynamic equilibrium between Western symmetry and Japanese "occult balance." For a garden built in earthquake country directly above the Hayward Fault, balance is a critical feature.

The architectural structures combine Japanese motifs with the sturdy simplicity of "California patio" design.

The beauty of Japanese-style gardens
is often found in their details; here a simple,
string-tied "fence" sets off the elegance of
black beach stones.

The Earl Burns Miller Japanese Garden
Long Beach, California

Small Japanesque gardens were constructed on university and college campuses from the 1920s, but it was only from 1960 that educational institutions constructed large-scale gardens. The function of these gardens is generally threefold: to augment the serene ambience of the North American college campus; to provide a living botanical laboratory; and to signal multiculturalism. The construction of an Asian garden may have been generally perceived as a positive step toward recognition of non-Western cultures in the 1960s, but by the 1980s heightened sensitivity to representations of ethnic identity made such gardens politically volatile spaces where the presence of a Japanese garden mattered less than whose power it reflected.

After the death of her first husband, Earl Burns Miller, Lorraine Miller Collins donated money to make a garden in the memory of the husband who had shared her interest in collecting Japanese art and visiting Japan. Miller gave $350,000 to California State University at Long Beach, where she knew the president and the chief landscape architect Edward R. Lovell, who was asked to design the garden. Lovell, with no experience in Japanese garden design, visited Kyoto with Miller, studied photos, examined gardens in Southern California, and consulted briefly with Kōichi Kawana—a landscape designer and well-known lecturer on Japanese gardens. This crash course resulted in a 1.3-acre garden built from 1979 to 1981 and featuring a smorgasbord of styles and design features. A central koi pond is surrounded by a wheelchair-accessible strolling path and traversed by a gently arched bridge on the east and by a railed zigzag bridge on the west. At the back of the garden a bulky tile-roofed teahouse sits on a small hill, and, in the northwest corner, a stone and sand garden with moss and a small pine is enclosed by a shrubbery hedge. The small garden is filled with a variety of plants including willows, pines, azaleas, camellias, and nandina, as well as such standard ornaments as stone lanterns, a water basin, a miniature pagoda and Buddhist statues. A large waterfall and a broad shore of black beach stones further contribute to the visual density of the garden.

*The zigzag and arched bridges
are favorite photo spots
for the wedding parties that frequently use
the garden.*

Before the garden was completed it became the focus of a protest by the university's Asian American students and faculty led by Lloyd Inui, director of the Asian American Studies Program. Inui and others criticized the inauthenticity of the garden, represented by the artificial, concrete-cast rocks, overly dramatic waterfall, and general lack of sensitivity. At the heart of the controversy was the fact that the Caucasian designer, patron, and university administrators had planned a garden representing Japanese tradition without consulting or inviting the participation of the local Japanese American community. The critics were temporarily mollified when the university agreed to call it a garden "in the Japanese style" rather than a "Japanese Garden." And the crisis was finally resolved, and the name "Japanese Garden" returned, when Kawana—who had anonymously savaged the garden in newspaper accounts of the protest—was hired and given $125,000 to rebuild the waterfall, add real stones, change some plantings, and place lanterns and oversize bonsai at the entry gate. As much as the aesthetics of his improvements, it was Kawana's status in the Japanese American community that mollified claims for authenticity. In short, what mattered was not so much the authenticity of Kawana's garden design, but his authenticity as a Japanese.

Despite its fractious birth amidst aesthetic criticism and ethnic academic politics, the Miller Garden has matured into one of the most widely utilized and socially conscious gardens in North America. In addition to raising revenue for its upkeep through rental for weddings and photo sessions, it is used for university art

courses, recreation and leisure studies classes, and reading and writing labs. Community groups which regularly visit include the Braille Institute, the V.A. hospital and school classes of all grades (notably fourth graders who utilize it for a unit on Asia). The garden hosts Japanese American organizations and Japanese culture groups including local koi, *ueki* tree trimming, ikebana, bonsai and tea ceremony clubs. Other cultural activities include a Girls' Day festival in early March, Boys' Day celebration in early May, Japanese Story and Arts Day in mid-summer, Harvest Moon nocturnal tour in September, and Chrysanthemum Festival in October. In addition, the garden hosts seasonal horticultural activities.

Although the garden is small, viewing platforms such as this (above) afford picturesque vistas across the koi-stocked pond (overleaf).

The Japanese Garden
at the Tillman Water Reclamation Plant
Van Nuys, California

Given the great popularity and adaptability of Japanese-style gardens, it is not surprising to find them at universities, museums, civic centers, and even hospitals across North America. Nonetheless it is only in California that one finds Suihōen (Garden of Water and Fragrance) constructed at the Donald C. Tillman Water Reclamation Plant in the Sepulveda Flood Control Basin in Los Angeles' San Fernando Valley. Located next to a sewage treatment facility and abutting architect Anthony Lumsden's futuristic Administration Building, the garden attempts a balancing act between faithful copying and creative adaptation.

Tillman, chief water engineer for the Municipal Water District of the City of Los Angeles, was fascinated with Japanese gardens and enrolled in Kōichi Kawana's adult education classes on Japanese garden history and Japanese art at UCLA Extension. In the late 1970s, Tillman commissioned Kawana to design a garden to show the public how they may profitably use reclaimed water from a new $75-million facility. The 6.5-acre garden, dedicated in 1984, rings three-quarters of a large pond, which takes up roughly half of the total acreage. The remaining side of the island-dotted and carp-filled pond is fronted by the Administration Building. Despite its high-tech finish, the building suggests the modular rigor of the Japanese *sukiya* architecture used at Katsura Villa and in other Edo-period stroll gardens. Immediately east of the garden is a sewage treatment plant, which makes the garden's name ironic on warm days when the breeze blows to the west carrying the pungent aroma of the adjacent facility. Although garden pamphlets describe an "authentic" garden, Kawana adapts elements from Japan's famous Edo-period (1615–1868) stroll gardens to fit the Southern California climate and the inescapably modern context of the garden, creating what is arguably the most successful of his several large and dramatic pond-centered gardens.

Inside the tile-roofed entry gate just west of the administration building, Kawana locates his most abstract element, a dry garden with stones and shrubs placed in gravel raked to suggest waves in the sea. In the center a large turf-covered mound, planted with pines, shrubs, and stones, is meant to represent the tortoise island, symbolic of longevity. A wisteria arbor is tucked into the southwest corner of the garden. A broad, wheelchair-accessible path skirts the side of the pond while another curves picturesquely among grassy hillocks planted with mock orange and pines and set with large stones. As the paths converge halfway along the pond, the

While the main paths around the garden are handicap-accessible, decorative stepping stones convey the impression of the Japanese stroll gardens on which it was modeled.

hills and shrubs give way to allow dramatic views of the scenic islands and the distant pavilions across the pond—effects culled from such gardens as Katsura Villa and Kōrakuen. Other reused motifs from Kyoto gardens include the boat landing stones of hand-hewn granite from Shūgakuin, the pebble-covered beach from the Sento Palace, and from Heian Shrine both the pond crossing made by circular mill stones and the zigzag, eight-planked *yatsuhashi* bridge through an iris marsh. More original is a pond inlet, in the garden's northwest corner, where Kawana attempts to modernize the *Amanohashidate* (floating bridge of heaven) motif from Katsura by constructing a long stone-walled spit of land planted with pines.

At the northern end of the pond a long, arched wooden bridge leads to the shoin pavilion cantilevered over the pond. An adjoining 4.5-tatami-mat teahouse includes a waiting arbor (*machiai*) and *roji* garden with requisite stepping stones, sleeve-fence, and water basin. The wood-shingled, hipped-and-gabled *shoin* is modified inside with a food service area and may be rented for parties or meetings. East of the *shoin*, a small hill covered with pygmy bamboo broken up by stones, cycads, and azaleas is surmounted by a rustic shelter open on two sides to allow clear unfettered views across the pond. To the rear a cascade rushes between a channel of stones. The path forks to lead to the *yatsuhashi* in the iris marsh or to make an s-curve through an extended field of black beach stones bordered on the east by a ground cover of viburnum, which blooms white in the spring. Both paths culminate at the administration building. Throughout the garden are several types of stone lanterns. More unusual are the numerous banks of clipped shrubs, primarily varieties of pittosporum. Although Japanese maple, yew, plum, and cherry are planted, more distinctive are the conifers, which range from black pines to coast redwoods.

Magnolia (overleaf) are but one of the
fifteen major tree species,
both Japanese and North American,
at the garden.

Anthony Lumsden's futuristic
Administration Building (below)
adds an otherworldly element
and screens the garden from the
attached sewage treatment plant.

Japanese Friendship Garden of San Diego
San Diego, California

Like most gardens built through sister city organizations, the Japanese Friendship Garden of San Diego claims to capture the essence of Japanese culture—a "sense of harmonic oneness between Man and Nature" in the words of garden pamphlets—and to serve as an emblem of goodwill between America and Japan. These transcendent claims of beauty and peace conceal the long and intense political maneuvering required to create a symbolic civic landscape. The garden's genesis began in 1955 when the old Japanese Tea Pavilion, built for the 1915 Panama-California Exposition, was torn down for zoo expansion. When the San Diego–Yokohama Sister City Society formed in 1957, member Will Hippen proposed an "authentic" Japanese garden as a symbol of international friendship and to make amends to the Japanese American community. In 1959 two concessionaires from San Francisco's Japanese Tea Garden petitioned San Diego for permission to build a commercial teahouse in Balboa Park, but they soon pulled out. Hippen persisted and, in 1968, after receiving permission from the Parks and Recreation Department for a site in Balboa Park, he placed a gate there in memory of deceased Mayor Chester Dail and solicited a garden plan from Kōichi Kawana.

In 1974, after city money was designated, the local landscape design firm Wimer, Yamada, Iwanaga and Associates was selected but later disqualified when a judge ruled that conflict of interest barred Wimmer's firm from the contract because he sat on the Park Board. In 1976 the city chose another firm based on Takeo Uesugi's plan for a six-part garden to be built in stages. However, they debated the inclusion of a teahouse—a feature Uesugi felt was inappropriately commercial in a garden dedicated to presenting a living example of Japanese art and commemorating the Japanese American community. In 1978 the Japanese Friendship Garden Society of San Diego was formed to solicit funds. Despite the tireless efforts of several

In the rear garden, designer Ken Nakajima's dramatic arrangement of large stones recalls his gardens in Japan as well as in Montreal and Houston.

*An unusual
feature of the garden is the
Kōetsu-style sleeve fence placed
in a bed of raked gravel.*

devoted volunteers and the hiring of professional fundraisers, little money was received. Although annual pan-Asian culture festivals between 1981 and 1983 roused public support, only the 1984 gifts of $500,000 from Kyocera Corporation and $100,000 from its president allowed for a garden. Yet Society leadership still disagreed on the necessity of a commercially-oriented building and scrapped Uesugi's design for a new one by Takeshi (Ken) Nakajima, head of Tokyo-based Consolidated Garden Research, Inc. and planner of gardens for several world's fairs. Nakajima, working with San Diego architectural and landscape firms with Japanese American partners, was asked to design a small garden that could be built cheaply and quickly so that money could be raised for the more elaborate garden planned for the canyon behind the site. In-fighting again stymied progress until the city presented the Friendship Garden Society with $2 million in 1988.

In 1989, twenty-one years after placement of the Dail Gate, ground was broken for Nakajima's sand-and-stone garden (*sekitei*) and a Japanese-style "Exhibition House" in a garden now named Sankeien (Garden of the Three Ravines) after the famous namesake in Yokohama. The Exhibition House, built in the *sukiya* (or tea ceremony) style, features various art objects, a snackbar, and a giftshop as well as the best location from which to view the rear garden composed of imported black stones embedded in raked gravel. The house is approached by a long, curved path between two hedges of sunburst locust, several types of bamboo, and xylosma. Five different types of bamboo fences—perhaps the most unusual and beautiful aspects of the garden—are placed to the front and to the side of the house. The rear *sekitei* follows the minimalist design associated with Kyoto's famous Ryōanji and also found at Nakajima's garden at the Gyokudō Museum near Tokyo. The side gardens, in contrast, depart from standard form by including two lanterns among the stones. Upon its opening in 1990, the garden cost about $1.2 million dollars to complete, with the remaining parts of Nakajima's plan estimated at well over $12 million. As a result, in 1994 the board of the Friendship Garden Society decided to jettison Nakajima's lavish canyon garden project and instead rehire Uesugi to design an observation deck and food service area overlooking the canyon. The plan led to resignations from the society's board as well as a column in the *San Diego Union* asking citizens to choose the "true Japanese garden" over this "quick 'Jack-in-the-Box' tea garden." While the garden may have generated friendship between San Diego and Yokohama, it was less successful among those responsible for it.

*This Ryōanji-style fence (above)
is one of several beautiful bamboo fences.*

*The formal geometry of the entry garden
(overleaf) contrasts with the informal
naturalness of the rear garden
(see photo p. 143).*

*The side garden (left) presents
a creative mix of a water basin and lantern
associated with a tea garden,
Kinkakuji-style fence,
and Zen-style stones set in sand.*

At the center of the large garden
a waterfall-fed pond (above) is viewed from
a restaurant designed to resemble a Japanese-style pavilion.

San Diego Tech Center
San Diego, California

Just as Japanese design has been often linked theoretically to modern architecture, Japanese garden art has been considered appropriate for landscaping office buildings because of this landscape style's ostensible modernism and cost-efficient minimalism (supposedly requiring little upkeep). Japanese gardens also enunciate a cultural transnationalism that parallels modern multinational corporate culture. The first "corporate Japanese garden" was built in 1952 by Isamu Noguchi for the Reader's Digest Building in Tokyo, and subsequent gardens have appeared in various forms in the following decades at the corporate headquarters of Deere and Company in Moline, Illinois, and Gulf States Paper Corporation in Tuscaloosa, Alabama. The largest and most successful example is the San Diego Tech Center. Built in the office park corridor at Sorrento Mesa in north San Diego County, the "garden" occupies the center of a thirty-acre business park developed by Jack Naiman in 1982. Constructed at a cost of about $5 million, the garden accommodates a fitness center, swimming pool, tennis and volleyball courts, half-mile jogging trail, and dining pavilion in a five-and-a-half-acre rectangle bounded by three steel-gray office buildings. Naiman, a visionary developer, wanted to return humanity to the modern workplace by spending millions of dollars to transform a piece of soulless industrial real estate into a realm of tranquillity and craftsmanship—creating what *Newsweek* cited as one of the "Offices of the Future." Through this holistic design, Naiman sought to lure corporate clients into the office space by providing an environment conducive to a harmonious life balancing work, physical fitness, and mental health.

Naiman hired Japanese-born and trained landscape architect Takeo Uesugi to create a "place of peace and tranquillity" fusing elements of Japanese garden design with a series of landscapes reflecting the natural topography of the San Diego region. The latter is manifest in the suggestion of mountains, rivers, and ocean through masses of native trees as well as stones and a large pond. Groupings of native cedar, redwood, and Torrey pine as well as Japanese maples, gingko, and bamboo ease the transitions between the massive buildings and the smaller scale of the central garden elements. Together with artificial hills, the groves of trees also help divide the large garden into intimate sections. Planted along the numerous curving stroll paths, the trees are integral to the hide-and-reveal technique adapted from Edo-period stroll gardens. Uesugi harmonizes the Japanesque garden with the modern glass and steel architecture by treating the edges of the landscape as transitional natural spaces created by dense plantings without garden ornaments. At the

To hide such unwanted features as the rear of buildings or a tennis court, designer Takeo Uesugi arranged screens of shrubs and bamboo .

mirrored-glass entrance to the southern building a large granite stone functions both as a piece of abstract modern sculpture and as a bridge to the adjacent dry garden. Nearby are several low grass-covered hillocks dotted with stones and cleaved by a "dry river" composed of gravel and punctuated by several more granite boulders. Here Uesugi radically enlarges the "dry garden" concept, and adapts the tradition of creating miniature mountains common in stroll gardens, in order to suggest the rolling, boulder-strewn hills and arroyos of Southern California.

Despite the synthetic nature of Uesugi's designs, which usually strives for translation rather than authenticity, the landscape is dominantly Japanese in tone. Placed throughout the garden are several stone lanterns and other ornaments. The buildings by the pool and courts are Japanese in style with white plaster walls as well as shingle or tile roofs. The same style is used for the dining pavilion—the landscape's geographic and scenic center. The pavilion garden is the only area that attempts to capture the look of an "authentic" Japanese garden. The pavilion is cantilevered over a large koi pond fed by a waterfall (and a dry stream). Guests, whether seated inside or outside on the verandah, see only the garden as plantings along a large hill screen out the surrounding buildings. A low, arched bridge to a rocky island, stone pagoda, and *yukimi*-style lantern complete the stereotypical Japanese scenery.

While Japanese-style gardens make sense when placed at the offices of Japanese companies, such as the Mazda and Nissan offices south of Los Angeles, or in the former Japan Airlines Terminal at Los Angeles International Airport, it is testimony to the Asian orientation of the West Coast that Japanesque gardens are found at the Nike corporate complex in Portland, the Weyerhauser headquarters near Tacoma, and the Port Authority of Seattle.

*Uesugi's artful placement
of stones and shrubs makes the pond seem
convincingly natural.*

The Golden Door

Escondido, California

Spirituality is central to the appeal of Japanese-style gardens in America. In a culture ever more reliant on technology and maintaining an increasingly frenetic pace, Japanese gardens represent a therapeutic retreat into the timeless beauty of traditional Japan. When Deborah Szekely set out in the late 1960s to rebuild her Golden Door spa in Escondido, California, she sought to adapt the features of a classic Japanese *honjin* inn where guests receive physical, spiritual, and aesthetic sustenance. Although the idea for a Japanese retreat grew directly from Szekely's interests in Zen, Japanese art, and natural food, construction of the new Golden Door evolved through the efforts of several persons. First, Szekely and San Diego architect Robert Mosher traveled to Japan to study architecture and gardens— Miyajima, Katsura Villa, and Ryōanji left the deepest impressions—by staying at twenty-one inns in twenty-five nights. Next, Szekely met Lennox Tierney, then Asian art curator at the San Diego Museum of Art and noted lecturer on gardens, who served as her "aesthetic adviser." After Mosher's firm constructed the deep-eaved tile-roofed buildings of the new Golden Door complex, local landscaper Kinya Washio installed a temporary garden. In 1975 Takendo Arii began seven years of careful garden construction. Arii, a student of Jūki Iida, had worked on the Japanese garden at Seaworld, but this was his first major commission.

The Golden Door is composed of ten acres of low Japanese-style pavilions and gardens tucked at the base of an oak-covered hillside along a small stream. The creative adaptation of Japanese garden features is established in the parking area by two Kasuga lanterns set amidst gravel and stones. Across the road a gatehouse leads to a bridge, which, after spanning Deer Springs Creek, leads to the main office. This structure, decorated with Japanese art, opens onto the lushly landscaped grounds. Several different garden styles are situated in the large rectangular areas between the central buildings (containing offices, gym, dining hall, and other communal rooms) and in the more irregular spaces between these buildings and the detached guest bungalows on the hill. In the geometric central court, composed of sloping lawn planted with several types of shrubs and pines, Arii placed a dry stream bed and a bell tower used to call guests to dinner. To the east, at the bottom of the

The great beauty and tranquillity of the garden at the Golden Door are visible only after one passes through several symbolic gates and doors.

hillside and the corner of two perpendicular structures, lies a pool. At its far side is a stage platform used for fashion shows and other performances. The pond is fed by a beautiful meandering stream, which drops among rocks and shrubs from the cluster of guest bungalows on the hill. In the confined rectangular courtyard between these rooms, Arii placed an abstract dry garden of rocks set in raked sand. A small "personal garden," behind each hill-facing room, complements the Japanese decor inside.

The gardens are dotted with lanterns, water basins, and small Buddhist statues to create different focal points and to heighten the feeling of being in a magical, foreign environment. Stepping stones and aggregate stone walkways (*nobedan*) carefully control one's pace and suggest different levels of formality. For all his faithfulness to Japanese design principles, Arii balances tradition and originality in the prominence given native plants, local stones, and the creative adaptation of such traditional features as the sleeve-fences (*sodegaki*). The garden not only creates an exotic environment of elegant serenity, but is central to the Golden Door philosophy of "creating order from disorder." The change in one's outer world necessary to change the "inner world" is accentuated by "oriental" activities including a garden tour, yoga, t'ai chi, meditation, flower arrangement, and, during special "Inner Door" retreats, raking the stone-and-sand garden. Expansion plans call for a new entry garden, a larger pond with island, and an independent meditation hall.

*The platform on the pond
is used for performances of Japanese music and
for fashion shows.*

*The lotus-shaped water basin
is one of many stone ornaments
placed throughout the garden
to encourage brief pauses
during a stroll.*

James Irvine Garden
Los Angeles, California

The garden is designed around two streams and a small pond, which are said to symbolize the different experiences of three generations of Japanese Americans.

Japanese Americans first built gardens for themselves in the decade before World War II. In the 1950s and early 1960s Japanese American Buddhist temples often featured garden landscapes. Yet it was not until the late 1960s and 1970s, with the rise of the "ethnic pride" movement, that Japanese American civic groups began to create gardens to celebrate directly their culture and history in North America. Among the growing number of such gardens, the James Irvine Garden at the Japanese American Cultural and Community Center in the Little Tokyo district of Los Angeles is the most notable both in design and symbolism. It serves as a green space for residents and workers in Little Tokyo and as a symbolic place for members of the larger Japanese American community.

Upon the founding of the Japanese American Cultural and Community Center (JACCC) in 1974, organization leaders felt that a garden would be an appropriate addition to their planned six-story center. President George J. Doizaki was particularly interested in a garden and enlisted the help of Tom Yanase, president of the California Landscape Contractors Association's Pacific Coast Chapter, as well as the Southern California Gardeners' Federation and Centinela Chapter of the California Association of Nurserymen. Two grants totaling $250,000 from the James Irvine Foundation kicked off the garden's fundraising, with $150,000 more contributed in cash and in-kind donations by Japanese American individuals and businesses. Takeo Uesugi—an Osaka-born landscape architect and associate professor in the department of landscape architecture at California Polytechnic University, Pomona—was chosen to design the garden based on his work in Japan and his plans for the Friendship Garden in San Diego's Balboa Park. Built between May 1978 and December 1979, the garden was constructed by more than two hundred volunteers who hauled 250 tons of stone from Mt. Baldy and planted more that $40,000 worth of donated shrubs and trees. Since the garden was dedicated on March 2, 1980, local gardeners and others have continued to volunteer for the semi-annual "Root for JACCC" pruning and clean-up days.

Uesugi met the design challenge posed by the small (8,500 square feet) triangular site by adapting Jihei Ogawa's famous Murin'an garden in Kyoto. A waterfall issues from the rear corner of the sloping garden, commencing a 170-foot stream that divides into two parts then reunites in a shallow pool at the garden's bottom. The garden can be circumambulated by a path that leads from the entry door at the garden's base, crosses the rivulet on an earthen bridge, ascends to the

*Located one story below ground level
and overlooked by residential and business towers, the Irvine
Garden is an oasis of calm in a harsh urban setting.*

waterfall, then continues back to the garden's base, where a large, formal wooden-railed bridge spans the broadening stream. Although two turf-covered hillocks form the central focal point of the garden, in the manner of Murin'an, the garden features low plantings of native and Japanese species including azalea, heavenly bamboo, mock orange, Indian hawthorne, golden bamboo, camellia, natal plum, shiny xylosma, and Oregon grape, while trees including camphor, Japanese maple, zelkova, black pine, several types of magnolia, and coast redwood serve as visual highlights or to partially screen out some of the surrounding buildings. Several stone lanterns, a water basin, and two sleeve-fences (*sodegaki*) provide distinctly Japanese ornamentation. Stone placement was supervised by Uesugi's teacher Dr. Tadashi Kubo of Osaka University.

Uesugi named the garden Seiryū-en (Garden of the Clear Stream) to empha-size the symbolic importance of the watercourse. According to the designer, through the "lifeline" of the stream the garden represents the generational evolution of Japanese Americans: the cascade is emblematic of the tribulations of the immigrant issei (first generation) against cultural and economic barriers; the split stream symbolizes the conflict experienced by nisei (second generation) divided by questions of national and cultural allegiance during World War II; and, finally, the quiet pool represents the hope for the peaceful experience of future generations. While the water in fact is pumped back to the top of the garden, conceptually it runs out of the garden to the city beyond, indicating the ideal of becoming part of the American community. The spirit of synthesis and adaption led Uesugi to call this "a Japanese American garden, but with the spirit and principles of a Japanese garden."

California Scenario
Costa Mesa, California

Almost all Japanese-style gardens in North America call themselves "Japanese" and deploy the superficial emblems—lanterns, bridges, ponds, clipped pines—of most premodern gardens in Japan. Yet, from the 1980s a handful of landscape designers have constructed gardens that adapt elements of Japanese design but downplay or abjure altogether the external symbols of Japanese gardens. The archetype for these designers is the Japanese American artist Isamu Noguchi (1904–88), who over four decades constructed a half-dozen gardens synthesizing elements from Japanese landscape, modern Western sculpture, and stage design. In the 1958 Jardin Japonais at UNESCO in Paris, Noguchi's work is "Japanese" by declaration. But even in his gardens at the Reader's Digest Building, Tokyo, 1951, for CIGNA, Bloomfield Hills, Connecticut, 1957, at Beinecke Library of Yale University, 1964, and at Chase Manhattan Bank Plaza, New York, 1964, Noguchi reformulates Japanese garden design within the context of modernist sculpture, although no such designation is given and all Japanese garden ornaments are excluded. California Scenario, at the South Coast Plaza Town Center in Costa Mesa, California, is Noguchi's last, largest, and most interactive garden space, fusing elements from static rock gardens with the temporal and spatial qualities of stroll gardens.

When developer Henry Segerstrom commissioned Noguchi to design a fountain for a small park in 1980, he gave the famous sculptor free artistic rein. Noguchi then asked to create a tribute to the ecologies of California in the entire 1.6-acre area between two glass office towers and the L-shaped, forty-foot-high rear walls of a parking structure. The space is composed around six distinct "elements" and one sculpture titled "Spirit of the Lima Bean." Made of fifteen large, brown decomposed granite stones cut and fitted at Noguchi's studio in Takamatsu, Japan, it symbolizes the agricultural heritage of both California and the Segerstrom family (who owned bean fields in the area). Next to the sculpture rises "Forest Walk," a rectangular hillside rimmed by redwoods, entered by a U-shaped path of Sierra white granite, and planted in the center with wild flowers and grasses. To the north the "Energy Fountain," a water-spouting, stainless steel cylinder set in a cone of granite, represents the vitality that Noguchi associated with the state in which he was born. The heart of the garden is the rectangle directly in front of the two white walls: here Noguchi dynamically balances geometric and organic shapes, stone, steel, plants, and water in a way that recalls his stage sets for Martha Graham even as it evokes a surrealist Japanese garden. The ensemble of forms and spaces is bounded to the

north by "Land Use," an eight-foot-high oval knoll of honeysuckle inset with a tomblike slab of white granite. Near the intersection of the two walls at the garden's opposite side is "The Desert Land," a low, circular mound of gravel planted with six desert plant species. The spiny forms of the cactus seem entirely sculptural in the context of the other objects. Between the desert circle and the oval mound Noguchi set a thirty-foot-tall triangle of sandstone, titled "Water Source," and resembling the Jantar Mantar observatory in Jaipur, India. From its apex water flows into a winding stream, set with small stones resting on a bed of gravel, and seemingly cut into the sandstone "ground" of the garden. The watercourse, flanked by six decomposed granite boulders, culminates in a polished white granite pyramid abstractly emblematic of its title, "Water Use." Placed around the garden are white granite benches as well as trash containers and ash trays of the same material carved to suggest a type of formal water basin (*chōzubachi*) used in many Japanese gardens.

The three-dimensional triangle representing "Water Use" (below) recalls the large buildings constructed for astronomical projections by the Mughal rulers of India.

California Scenario has been criticized by some landscape architects for lacking the sequential unfolding of vistas central to stroll gardens as well as the calibrated relation of objects in Zen-temple stone gardens. One critic termed it not an open space but an art object stretched over an empty space. Yet, California Scenario is a place for contemplation, in the manner of Zen stone gardens, and an active space of changing scenes like a stroll garden. In addition to its planned use by workers on break, sightseers, and even performers, the garden has been adopted by such unsanctioned users as nocturnal skateboarders and local "witches" drawn to this unconventional and challenging space in the otherwise blandly rational urban fabric of Orange County. Here, the essence of Japanese garden design thrives, even as the external features have been discarded.

The garden is designed
to be strolled through and to be seen
from the two office towers that bound it on
the north and the east.

Noguchi elegantly juxtaposes
the artificial and the organic (overleaf)
to evoke the dramatic beauty
and the dynamic spirit
of California.

Japanese Tea Garden at Golden Gate Park

Hagiwara Tea Garden Drive, San Francisco, California
(415) 666-7107
Hours: open daily, hours vary by season. Fee.
Designed by George Turner Marsh, Makoto Hagiwara,
Nagao Sakurai.

Bibliography

Brown, Kendall H. "Rashōmon: the multiple histories of the Japanese Tea Garden at Golden Gate Park." *Studies In The History of Gardens and Designed Landscapes* 18:2 (April–June 1998): 93–119.

Ishihara, Tanso, and Gloria Wickham. *The Japanese Tea Garden in Golden Gate Park 1893–1942*. Privately published, 1979.

McClintock, Elizabeth. *The Japanese Tea Garden, Golden Gate Park, San Francisco, California*. San Francisco: The John McClaren Society, 1977.

San Francisco Recreation and Parks Department. *Japanese Tea Garden, Golden Gate Park*. Undated pamphlet.

The Huntington Japanese Gardens

1151 Oxford Road, San Marino, California
(626) 405-2141
Hours: Tuesday to Friday 12:00–4:30, Saturday and Sunday 10:30–4:30.
Stroll garden designed by William Hertrich; "Zen garden" designed by Robert Watson.

Bibliography

Brandow, Anita. *Guide to the Henry Edwards Huntington Botanical Gardens*. San Marino, Calif.: Henry E. Huntington Library and Art Gallery, 1971.

Garret, Peter. *Stately Homes of California*. Boston: Little, Brown & Co.: 1915.

Hertrich, William. *The Huntington Botanical Gardens 1905 . . . 1949, Personal Recollections of William Hertrich*. San Marino, Calif.: Henry E. Huntington Library and Art Gallery, 1988 (reprint).

"Huntington Is Buyer of Garden." *Pasadena Star* (October 19, 1911): 1.

Lancaster, Clay. *The Japanese Influence in America*. New York: Abbeville Press, 1983 (reprint).

"Prize For Huntington." *Pasadena Daily News* (August 19, 1911): 1.

San Marino League Committee of Docents for the Japanese Garden. *Japanese Garden of the Henry E. Huntington Library and Art Gallery*. Privately published, n.d.

Thorpe, James. *Henry Edwards Huntington, A Biography*. Berkeley: University of California Press, 1994.

Hakone Gardens

21000 Big Basin Way, Saratoga, California
(408) 741-4994
Hours: weekdays 10:00–5:00, weekends 11:00–5:00.
Fee for parking.
Designed by Naoharu Aihara; Bamboo Garden by Kiyoshi Yasui.

Bibliography

Fox, Frances L. *Hakone Gardens, A Charming Bit of Nippon Is Authentically Portrayed in Quaint Saratoga City Park*. San Jose, Calif.: Harlan-Young Press, 1968.

"Hakone debt worries officials." *San Jose Mercury News* (November 20, 1993): B-1.

Ishihara, Tanso, and Gloria Wickham. *Hakone Garden*. Kyoto: Kawahara shoten, 1974.

Kubota Garden

Renton Avenue South and Fifty-fifth Avenue South, Seattle, Washington
(206) 725-5060
Hours: open daily during daylight.
Designed by Fujitarō Kubota.

Bibliography

Shibata, Yoshimi. "The Garden That Love Built." *Reader's Digest* (March 1989): 79–83.

Robinson, Thomas M. "Traditions in Translation: The Gardens of Fujitarō Kubota." Master's thesis, University of Washington, 1992.

Streatfield, David. "The Resonance of Japan in Pacific Northwest Gardens." *Washington Park Arboretum Bulletin* 60:1 (Winter 1998): 2–5.

The Bloedel Reserve

7571 Northeast Dolphin Drive, Bainbridge Island, Washington
(206) 842-7631
Hours (by reservation only): Wednesday to Sunday 10:00–4:00.
Pond garden designed by Fujitarō Kubota; dry and moss gardens designed by Kōichi Kawana.

Bibliography

Bloedel, Prentice. "The Bloedel Reserve: Its Purpose and Its Future." *University of Washington Arboretum Bulletin* 41:1 (Spring 1980): 2–6.

Brown, Richard. "The Japanese Garden: An Evolution in Time." *The Bloedel Reserve* 2:2 (Summer/Fall 1990): 1, 4.

Frey, Susan Rademacher. "A Series of Gardens." *Landscape Architecture* 74:5 (May 1986): 54–61, 128.

Haag, Richard. "Contemplations of Japanese Influence on the Bloedel Reserve." *Washington Park Arboretum Bulletin* 53:2 (Summer 1990), 16–19.

Lowry, Dèci. "The Moss Garden at Bloedel Reserve." *Pacific Horticulture* 51:1 (January 1990): 16–20.

The UCLA Hannah Carter Japanese Garden

10619 Bellagio Road, Los Angeles, California
(310) 825-4574
Hours (by reservation only): Tuesday 10:00–1:00, Wednesday 12:00–3:00.
Designed by Nagao Sakurai; reconstructed by Kōichi Kawana in 1969 after flood damage.

Bibliography

Benson, Sheila. "Japanese Garden . . . Where Peace Rules." *Los Angeles Times* (August 20, 1991): F-6, 7.

Goodman, Marilyn. "Garden of Inner Peace, Westwood, California." *Garden Design* 2:1 (Spring 1983): 42–43.

Guiberson, Gordon. *A Garden That Reminds One Of Kyoto*. San Francisco: Grabhorn Press, 1962.

"Images of Japan, The Orient in Bel-Air." *Architectural Digest* 34:4 (May/June 1977): 145–49.

"It's not Kyoto or Nikko, it's right in Los Angeles." *Sunset* (March 1966): 104–8.

The UCLA Hannah Carter Japanese Garden. Undated pamphlet.

Ganna Walska Lotusland

695 Ashley Road, Montecito, California
(805) 969-9990
Tours (by reservation only): mid-February through mid-November,

Wednesday to Saturday.
Designed by Frank Fujii and Osvald da Ros; additions by
Kōichi Kawana.

Bibliography
Dobins, Winifred Starr. *California Gardens*. New York:
Macmillan, 1931.
Myrick, David. *Montecito and Santa Barbara*. Glendale, Calif.:
Trans-Anglo Press, 1987 (vol. 1) and 1991 (vol. 2).
Walska, Ganna. *Always Room at the Top*. New York: Richard R.
Smith, 1945.

Washington Park Arboretum Japanese Garden

Lake Washington Boulevard East, north of East Madison Street,
Seattle, Washington
(206) 684-7050
Hours: daily from 10:00 A.M., closing times vary with season. Fee.
Designed by Jūki Iida.

Bibliography
Iida, Jūki. "The Japanese Garden at the University of
Washington." Translation of article published in Japanese in *Niwa* 12
(February 1974): 17–24.
Iida, Jūki, and Associates. "Our Japanese Garden." *Washington
Park Arboretum Bulletin* 23:4 (Winter 1960): 139–40.
Kruckenberg, Arthur R. "The Japanese Design Connection—
Northwestern Natives in the Japanese Garden." *Washington Park
Arboretum Bulletin* 60:1 (Winter 1998): 14–18.
Medbury, Scott. "The Once and Future Japanese Garden."
Washington Park Arboretum Bulletin 53:2 (Summer 1990): 2.
Sorrels, Kenneth. "Jūki Iida on Building the Japanese Garden."
Washington Park Arboretum Bulletin 53:2 (Summer 1990): 6–10.

Nitobe Memorial Garden, University of British Columbia

6501 Northwest Marine Drive, Vancouver, British Columbia
(604) 228-5858
Hours: mid-March to mid-October, daily 10:00–6:00; 10:00–4:00 at
other times. Fee.
Designed by Kannosuke Mori.

Bibliography
Hilborn, Ulrike. "The Nitobe Memorial Garden." *Washington Park
Arboretum Bulletin* 53 (Summer 1990): 14–18.
Mooney, Patrick. "Ecology of Mind in the Traditional Japanese
Garden." In *Nitobe Memorial Garden International Symposium
Proceedings* (1994): 12–17.
Neill, John W. "Nitobe Memorial Garden—History and
Development." *Davidsonia* 1:2 (Summer 1970): 10–15.

The Japanese Garden, Portland, Oregon

611 S.W. Kingston, Portland, Oregon
(503) 223-9233
Hours: open daily, times vary by season. Fee.
Designed by Takuma Tono.

Bibliography
Hamilton, Bruce Taylor. *Human Nature: The Japanese Garden
of Portland, Oregon*. Portland, Ore.: Japanese Garden Society of
Oregon, 1996.
Japanese Garden Society of Oregon. *The Garden Way: The Plan
of the Japanese Garden Society of Oregon*. Portland, Ore.: Japanese
Garden Society of Oregon, 1990.
Japanese Garden Society of Oregon. *The Plan for a Japanese
Garden in Oregon*. Portland, Ore.: Japanese Garden Society of
Oregon, 1965.
Japanese Garden Society of Oregon. *Symbolism &
Lanterns in the Japanese Garden*. Portland, Ore.: Japanese
Garden Society of Oregon, 1997.
"Japanese Gardens Dressed In Best For Easter
Sunday." *The Sunday Oregonian* (April 14, 1968): 3.
Jordan, Barbara. "Hilltop Garden Shows Beauty of
Japanese Landscaping." *The Sunday Oregonian* (March 28,
1971): D-1.

Japanese Friendship Garden, Kelley Park

Senter Road, between Story Road and Phelan Avenue, San
Jose, California
(408) 297-0778.
Hours: daily 10:00–sunset. Fee for parking.

Bibliography
Barrett, Dick. "Friendship Garden Well Worth Visiting."
San Jose News (July 28, 1971): 1, 21.
Conn, Kenneth S. "Real Tea House Opening in Kelley
Park Friday." *San Jose News* (July 30, 1970): 1–2.
Cummings, Clover. "New Japanese Garden: Friendship
Takes Tangible Form." *San Jose Mercury-News* magazine
(October 31, 1965): 10.
Doss, Margo Patterson. "Japanese Gardens and Old
San Jose." *San Francisco Chronicle* magazine (May 25,
1986): 6.
Gerlitz, Bert. "San Jose Builds A Japanese-American
Friendship Garden." *Western City* (May 1966): 33–34.
"Japanese to Help Dedicate Teahouse: 112-man
Delegation from Sister City." *San Jose News* (May 17,
1970): 1–7.

San Mateo Japanese Garden

Central Park, Laural and Fifth Avenue, San Mateo, California
(415) 377-4640.
Hours: Monday to Friday 10:00–4:00; Saturday and Sunday
11:00–4:00.
Designed by Nagao Sakurai.

Bibliography
Newman, Iva. " 'A Thing of Beauty.' " *San Mateo Times*
(August 21, 1966): 2A.
———. "The West looks East for serenity." *The San
Mateo Times* (April 17, 1981): 3.
Dennis, Julie. "City will celebrate Japanese Garden's
25th anniversary." *San Mateo Times* (August 21, 1991): 23.
Taylor, Joan Chatfield, and Melba Levick. *Visiting Eden:
The Public Gardens of Northern California*. San Francisco:
Chronicle, 1993.

Hayward Japanese Garden

City Center Drive at North Third Street, Hayward, California
(510) 881-6700.
Hours: daily 10:00–4:00.
Designed by Kimio Kimura.

Bibliography
Doss, Margo Patterson. "A Terrific New Garden." *San
Francisco Chronicle* magazine (March 27, 1985): 4.
Kimura, Kimio. "Japanese Landscape Design And It's
Applications." Master's thesis, University of California,
Berkeley, 1971.

Earl Burns Miller Japanese Garden,
California State University, Long Beach, California
(562) 985-8885
http://www.csulb.edu/~jgarden
Hours: Tuesday to Friday 8:00–3:30, Sunday 12:00–4:00.
Designed by Edward R. Lovell; revised by Kōichi Kawana.

Bibliography
Aronow, Ina. "A Cloud Darkens a Garden, Japanese-Style Creation Weathers Controversy." *Los Angeles Times* (January 5, 1982): D-1.

The Japanese Garden
at the Tillman Water Reclamation Plant
City of Los Angeles Donald C. Tillman Water Reclamation Plant, 6100 Woodley Avenue, Van Nuys, California
(818) 751-8166
Tours (by reservation only): Tuesday, Thursday, and Saturday mornings.
Designed by Kōichi Kawana.

Bibliography
De Wolfe, Evelyn. "Japanese Garden Uses Reclaimed Water." *Los Angeles Times* (May 16, 1993): K-6.
Kawana, Kōichi. *The Japanese Garden At The Donald C. Tillman Water Reclamation Plant*. Undated pamphlet.
———. "The Challenge of Building a Japanese Garden in the United States." In *Plants & Gardens, Brooklyn Botanic Garden Record: Japanese Gardens*. New York: Brooklyn Botanic Garden, 1990.

Japanese Friendship Garden of San Diego
Balboa Park, San Diego, California
(619) 232-2721
Hours: Tuesday, Friday, Saturday, and Sunday 10:00–4:00.
Designed by Ken Nakajima, Consolidated Garden Research, Inc.

Bibliography
Amero, Richard W. "Japanese Garden . . . Or Commercial Hodgepodge?" *San Diego Union-Tribune* (December 22, 1994): B-11.
Fong & LaRoca Associates. *Japanese Garden Master Plan, Balboa Park, San Diego, California*. Pamphlet, 1979.
"A new jewel in Balboa Park." *San Diego Tribune* (December 14, 1990): B-10.
Petitti, Nancy Murcko. "The Japanese Friendship Garden In Balboa Park: The Evolution Of An Idea." Master's thesis, San Diego State University, 1994.

San Diego Tech Center
9605 Scranton Road, San Diego, California
(619) 452-7960.
Hours: daily during daylight.
Designed by Takeo Uesugi & Associates.

Bibliography
Cleigh, Zenia. "Naiman creates environment that encourages humanity." *The San Diego Tribune* (November 10, 1983): C-1, 2.

The Golden Door
Escondido, California
(619) 744-5777
The garden is open only to spa guests.
Designed by Takendo Arii.

Bibliography
Berggren, Christine. "Sound of One Hand Clapping, New Japanese Gardens at The Golden Door." *San Diego Home/Gardener* (October 1983): 46–51.
Druse, Ken. "The Golden Door." *Garden Design* 3:4 (Winter 1984–85): 62–65.
The Golden Door. *The Sand Garden*. Pamphlet, 1986.
Mazzanti, Deborah Szekely. *Secrets of the Golden Door*. New York: William Morrow and Co., 1977.
Zigner, Gloria. "The Golden Door." *Orange Coast* (August 1994), 21–24.

James Irvine Garden,
Japanese American Cultural and Community Center
244 South San Pedro Street, Los Angeles, California
(213) 628-2725.
Hours: the garden can be viewed anytime from the plaza, and can be entered through the Japanese American Cultural and Community Center building, Monday to Saturday 9:00–5:00.
Designed by Takeo Uesugi & Associates.

Bibliography
Japanese American Cultural & Community Center. *James Irvine Garden*. Pamphlet, 1983.
Spiller, Jane. "A Secret Garden in Little Tokyo." *Los Angeles Times* (n.d.).

California Scenario, South Coast Plaza Town Center
Anton Street, between Avenue of the Stars and Park Center Drive, Costa Mesa, California
(714) 241-1700
Hours: daily 8:00–midnight.
Designed by Isamu Noguchi.

Bibliography
Ashton, Dore. *Noguchi East and West*. New York: Alfred A. Knopf, 1992.
Goldstein, Barbara. "California Scenario." *Arts and Architecture* 1:4 (n.d.): 16–20.
Herman, Ron. "A Question of Style and Purpose." *Process Architecture* 61 (August 1985): 105–6.
Johnson, Jory. "The Masques of Noguchi." *Landscape Architecture* 75:1 (January 1985): 58–64.
Noguchi, Isamu. *The Isamu Noguchi Garden Museum*. New York: Harry N. Abrams, 1989.
Walker, Peter. "A Levitation of Stones." *Landscape Architecture* 80:4 (April 1990): 57–59.
Winther, Bert. "Isamu Noguchi: The Modernization of Japanese Garden Design—Reduction, Exile, Abstraction." *Nihon teien gakkai shi* 1:1 (March 1993): 30–43.